Letters *to* Sam

Letters *to* Sam

———

A GRANDFATHER'S LESSONS ON LOVE, LOSS, AND THE GIFTS OF LIFE

Daniel Gottlieb

Sterling Publishing Co., Inc.
New York

Author's proceeds from the sale of this book are being donated to Cure Autism Now and other children's charities. For more information, visit www.cureautismnow.org.

Library of Congress Cataloging-in-Publication Data Available

10 9 8 7 6 5 4 3 2

Published by Sterling Publishing Co., Inc.
387 Park Avenue South, New York, NY 10016
© 2006 by Daniel Gottlieb
Distributed in Canada by Sterling Publishing
c/o Canadian Manda Group, 165 Dufferin Street
Toronto, Ontario, Canada M6K 3H6
Distributed in the United Kingdom by GMC Distribution Services
Castle Place, 166 High Street, Lewes, East Sussex, England BN7 1XU
Distributed in Australia by Capricorn Link (Australia) Pty. Ltd.
P.O. Box 704, Windsor, NSW 2756, Australia

Sterling ISBN-13: 978-1-4027-2883-9
        ISBN-10: 1-4027-2883-2

For information about custom editions, special sales, premium and corporate purchases, please contact Sterling Special Sales Department at 800-805-5489 or specialsales@sterlingpub.com.

*To my precious grandson Sam and
all the "Sams" in the world.
May their vulnerability open our hearts
so that they can find care and
we can find compassion.*

CONTENTS

Letters
to Sam

INTRODUCTION

Dear Reader,

When my precious grandson was born on May 25, 2000, my heart was filled with joy and love. Every grandparent knows these feelings and the special bond that, if we are lucky enough, we can share with a grandchild.

But in the years since Sam's birth, he and I have forged a bond with a difference.

You see, when Sam was born, I was a fifty-three-year-old man who had been a quadriplegic for twenty years. That's a long time to live with quadriplegia, as it takes quite a toll on one's body. I have been ill many times and, over the last couple of years, severely ill. So I didn't know if I would be lucky enough to have our relationship blossom over this many years. I didn't know if I would have the time to tell Sam all the things I'd observed from the unique perspective of my wheelchair.

My perspective is unusual for another reason: I have been practicing my craft of psychology for thirty-five years. I have watched people suffer, move on, and grow from the experience, while others have lived their lives stuck in their own pain. I have watched people confront their demons and open their hearts to estranged family members. They have taught me a great deal about courage, longing, and what it means to be human.

And it has been my luck to have other perspectives as well. During the last twenty years I have been hosting a psychology call-in radio show, *Voices in the Family*, broadcast from Philadelphia's NPR affiliate. I have heard tens of thousands of voices describe what they wish for, what they struggle with, and what they've mastered. Also, for the last ten years, I have been writing a column for the *Philadelphia Inquirer* and receiving dozens of letters every week from readers who want to share their thoughts and experiences.

Books taught me a bit about psychology. But paralysis taught me to sit still and keep my ears and heart open so I could listen.

From the moment that Sam was born, I knew I wanted to tell him about life and love and what it means to have parents who are vulnerable human beings. I wanted him to know about school. To see how important friends are and how mean they can be. I wanted to tell him about drugs and sex and romance and work and money and everything else.

I also wanted him to know me.

So that's how I started out these letters—wanting to tell Sam all of these things and more. I realized, of course, that it might be many years before he would have any genuine interest in what his grandfather wrote to him. But when I started these letters, I felt confident that—one way or another—Sam would someday read them.

Then, that expectation changed.

When Sam was just under two years old, his parents and I discovered that he showed signs of autism, the brain disorder that radically changes how a person perceives the world and relates to others—a disability that would change Sam's life. The discovery was heartbreaking for his mother, my child. I wept for her, not only because she was my child, but because she had already spent her childhood living with disability, and now she would spend the rest of her life living with it. And I wept for Sam. But I realized that I had even more now to tell him. Now I also wanted him to understand what it means to be "different" from everybody else. I wanted to teach him what I've learned about fighting against the kind of adversity that I face almost daily and that I fear he will face in his life. And I wanted to tell him how peace comes to us when we simply stop fighting.

Most of all, I wanted to tell Sam about love. I wanted him to know that Andrew Lloyd Webber got it right when he said, "Love changes everything." I wanted him to be fully loved and to savor every sensation that love elicits. And I wanted him to understand that as he gets older, giving love may be even more important than receiving it.

But in light of his autism, I had to wonder whether any of my words, wishes, expressions of love and observations on life would be meaningful to him. Autism takes many forms, and for any child in its hold, the future is unpredictable. If it turned out that Sam had the severest form, he might never be able to read or even comprehend what I wanted to communicate to him.

When Sam was first diagnosed, he had stopped babbling and was effectively mute. Over the next year and a half, he would bang his head on the floor when he got frustrated and would scream when he heard certain sounds. So I wondered: would he ever be able to read his grandfather's letters? But even though I had to ask that question, it did not deter me from writing on. Regardless of the extent of his disability, I had to tell my story and I had to express my love and devotion to this child. So, with hope as my constant companion, I almost assumed he would get the love and lessons I was trying to communicate. What concerned me far more was the possibility that I wouldn't have time to write all that I wanted to say.

And now, as it has turned out, I have been given that time.

Every chapter in this book is a letter to Sam. Some are stories about my life. Most are stories about what I've learned. All are stories about what it means to be human.

PART I

WELCOME TO THE WORLD

YOUR BIRTH

Dear Sam,

My life was changed the moment you were born. But your mother's life, my child's life, was changed even more.

When the time came for your birth, we knew your mother would be having a Cesarean section, and we all came to the hospital. There we were—your father, his mother, and me—hanging out in Debbie's hospital room, laughing nervously, waiting for the doctor to call her. As we waited, I had time to remember what it was like many years before when I waited in the hospital for your mother to be born, just eleven months after your aunt Ali. The moment each of my daughters came into the world, I made a promise to them, to myself, and to God that I would do everything in my power to protect my daughters and make their lives good. This is what almost all parents want for their children: a lifetime of happiness and an easy passage.

When your mother was a toddler, she had jet-black hair, adorable bangs, and big brown eyes. She and her big sister Ali were always together, holding hands. It seemed like Debbie was in Ali's shadow and content to be there. I have a picture on my desk of the two of them—ages four and three, on the beach, holding hands, taking care of each other as always.

Of course, they weren't always angels. One summer when we were on vacation, your grandmother Sandy and I put the girls to bed and went to sit out on the balcony. We thought we could enjoy the sunset in peace and quiet—but no such luck! Ali and Debbie just wouldn't settle down. Finally, I lost my temper. I went into their room and spanked each one of them, just one firm pat on each of their butts. But I'd never done anything like that—so they both cried. And so did I! There we were, the three of us, all crying and saying how sorry we were for what we'd done.

As a little girl, your mother always had the uncanny ability to climb inside my mind and heart and figure out what was going on in there. I remember the time, before my accident, when I took Debbie to the hospital to have a tonsillectomy. We were walking up and down in the hallway outside the operating room. She looked up at me and studied my expression.

"Daddy," she asked, "are you scared about my operation?"

In an effort to be honest with her, I said, "Yes, a little bit."

"What are you scared about?"

"Well," I said, "I'm scared they'll hurt your throat. And I guess I'm a little scared that even after the operation, you might still have trouble getting over your colds."

She shook her head. "That's not what you're scared of."

"Oh?" I looked down at her. "What, then?"

"You're scared I'm going to die in there."

Of course she was right. I had tried to tell her the things that I thought a little girl could hear, but she'd seen right through me to my real anxiety. How come she could always do that? I don't know!

Something similar happened shortly after my accident, when Debbie was six years old. I had just come home from the hospital, and I was feeling very insecure and unsure of myself personally as well as professionally. It was evening and the first patient I would see after my accident was about to arrive.

As I was sitting in my wheelchair outside Debbie's room, looking in the mirror (the only one in the house at wheelchair height), I started to comb my hair. (That was back when I had hair!) It was Debbie's bedtime. She was supposed to be sleeping. Instead, she came out of her room and stood beside me, watching.

Finally, very seriously, she said, "Daddy, why do you always worry about how you look before your patients come?"

"I don't know."

She reflected a moment. "It seems like you always have to look perfect."

"I don't know. I never thought about it." I was still trying to get my hair combed and beginning to feel uncomfortable about her probing questions.

"They're only people, you know."

Now I replied with a little more discomfort and animation. "I just don't know, Debbie. I never really thought about it."

"Well, think about it," she said, "and we'll talk about it in the morning."

With that, she went into her room and I went off to see my patient. Sure enough, I was up all night thinking about it. Once again, she had seen right through me!

But that little girl grew up, and in the years that followed, despite my commitment to protect her, she experienced a great deal of suffering. She lived in a home where, for reasons I'll tell you soon, she sometimes felt terrified and overwhelmed. As your mother grew through adolescence and adulthood, it seemed as if her pain began to accumulate. She still had her smile, but it did not seem so genuine. Her needs and wishes grew silent. Even her body began to look unwell as she got thinner, stayed out later at night, and lost the gleam in her eye.

That's why I was so happy, several years later, when she met your father and fell in love. When I first met him, I saw a kind man with a good heart who was also in love. And I got to know him, and I learned that he, like your mother, had suffered the consequences of a difficult childhood. Fortunately, both of your parents made a commitment to themselves not to let their past determine their future.

And then my child, your mother, told me that she was pregnant. She looked so happy and beautiful. All I could think was, "Another chance for joy!"

Debbie fervently researched motherhood. She wanted to know every detail of what she was experiencing, and she became my teacher. I would listen on the telephone, enthralled with her descriptions of what was happening. It was a blessed experience to watch her body grow with you.

When the time came, your father accompanied the doctor and your mother into the operating room while I went into the waiting room with your other grandmother. About ninety minutes later, your father came into the waiting room, crying. All he could say was, "It was awesome."

Soon we all went down the hall to meet you. Of course you were adorable, but what struck me most was what had happened to Debbie, my baby! In the two hours since I had seen her, she had become a mother—a different person. She seemed more calm, more present, and somehow older. Most of all, I saw a kind of happiness I had always wanted for her.

You are the product of the great love that two wounded souls have found. I love you every moment of every day. And I love you for the joy you have brought to my daughter.

Love,
Pop

———

RECLAIMING YOUR WISDOM

Dear Sam,

You and your parents both have jobs to do. Let's take a moment to talk about their job—and then yours.

Their job is to love you, protect you as best they can, try to understand you, and enjoy your laughter. I hope they will give you both roots and wings. When they give you roots, you will feel safe, loved, and secure, knowing they genuinely want to understand the person you are. When they give you wings, you will feel free to think whatever you want to think, free to explore the world of your heart and mind and the world outside.

Your job . . . well, I'll tell you what I think your job is.

Sam, there is a wonderful Jewish teaching that tells us that before a child is born, God infuses that child with all of the knowledge and wisdom he or she needs in life. Then God puts his finger to the child's lips and says, "shh," making at that moment a secret pact between the child and God. As the story goes, that's why everyone has that indentation on the upper lip. It's God's fingerprint.

But over time, that purity and wisdom get eroded. Children become socialized and shaped by experience. Life changes them into something different.

. . .

Several years ago, a middle-aged man with a heavy Italian accent came to my house to repair some windows. We talked for a while, and he seemed unusually bright and insightful. I wanted to get to know him a little better. When he told me he was Jewish, I got even more interested because I had never met a Jewish man with an Italian accent and an Italian last name.

As it turned out, he came from Rome. When he was a young man, he had wanted to become a rabbi. As he told me this, he turned reflective. "It's a funny thing about life," he said, gazing skyward. "I thought I would be a rabbi in Rome and instead, here I am repairing windows in New Jersey." He paused for a moment, then added, "I think we're born square and we die round."

So here's what I think, Sam. As the waters of life wash over us, we lose our sharp corners, and that can be good; we can take on surprising, satisfying new shapes. We can also lose some of the great wisdom that we were born with. But the evidence of that wisdom stays with us, right under our noses.

So your job is simply this: trust your instincts, remember your secret pact, and reclaim the wisdom you have always had.

Love,
Pop

LAP TIME

Dear Sam,

Looking back, I know I loved you from the moment of your birth. But for some reason it took about six months for my love to fully form. Early on, I loved "my grandson." After six months, I loved *you*. And I think something similar happened with your love for me.

I lived three hours away from you and your parents. I certainly wasn't available for bonding. And you didn't understand the concept of "grandfather" when you were just a baby. So at first you kept your distance from me. But everything changed at my father's funeral.

You were just six months old when he died, but we took you to the funeral. As I sat there quietly, all you wanted to do was climb up on my lap. It was as though you sensed my pain and wanted to be close to me. And since that time, whenever we are together, all you want to do is sit on my lap.

At first, I thought you were intrigued by the wheel-chair. But although that might be true, I don't think it's the whole story. I think at a certain level you know we are kindred spirits. You are beginning to see that I can't do what others do. In time you will really understand how different I am from everyone else. Part of my job with you is to teach you how to tolerate your own different-ness from other people and how to navigate your own waters.

As you get older, Sam, I will have more to say about how I've learned to cope with people staring at me or treating me differently. We can talk about fear, injustice, God, and the little gifts that sometimes live inside adversity.

But I believe there's another part of my job with you. I also have to make sure you never, ever forget what you knew at the age of six months. You knew to climb up on my lap.

Love,
Pop

YOUR PERFECTION

Dear Sam,

After you were born, I worried about your mother. I would call every day and ask her how you were, and every day she would say the same thing: "Sam is perfect." And that made me worry.

Sam, nobody is perfect. Each of us has imperfections that make us different from anyone else. I was afraid that if Debbie went on believing you were perfect, she would be hurt someday when your different-ness, whatever it was, became visible. And I was afraid that you would be hurt too.

That's why I struggled when I first noticed some unusual things that were happening in your development. You were about fourteen months old when I noticed that you weren't yet talking. You didn't seem to be paying attention to us when we talked to *you*. I thought there was a problem, but I didn't know how to tell your mother. What if I was fretting about problems that didn't exist? If I conveyed my anxiety to Debbie, I knew she would take my concerns seriously. But was that really fair? Why worry her unnecessarily if, in fact, I was just imagining things?

Despite these reservations, I finally did tell your mother

about my concerns. Of course, she and your father had both felt something was wrong, but like any parents, they hoped that they were just imagining things and that you would be fine.

At first we thought you might be deaf. I actually hoped that was the problem, because the other possibilities were so frightening: this could be a brain abnormality, mental retardation, or—autism. We banged pots and pans when you weren't looking, and often you did not turn around. But when we had your hearing tested, we found out it was just fine.

Then there were intelligence tests, behavior assessments, physical exams. Of course, we went to the best professionals we could find. The label they came up with was PDD—pervasive developmental disorder—which places you on the autism spectrum. The label alone didn't tell us much, but at least it gave us an explanation for the way you were acting. And though there are many things we do not know about this disorder, there are some things we do know.

Sam, you are adorable. I mean off-the-charts cute. Your smile can melt anybody's heart, and you are most capable of giving and receiving a great deal of love. All of these things will help you in your life. I also know how much you love me and how much you like to sit on my lap and ride with me in my wheelchair. These things will help me in *my* life! So now we know that you have your own personality, spirit, and soul, and that you improve the lives of those around you.

But we need to know more.

When you were first diagnosed, your parents and I did

everything we could to find out about PDD and autism. We learned that this disability inevitably steals something from children. We also learned that PDD would interfere with your ability to be flexible and to pick up social cues, as well as your fine motor dexterity. And we saw that you would have difficulty with too much stimulation. You would need some things in perfect order so that you could feel safe.

Autism has the power to steal opportunities for contact, intimacy, and love. In a strange paradox, if your autism were more severe, the opportunities you lose might hurt you less. But because your autism is not so severe, you may realize that you lack important skills for connecting with other people—you may be aware you are different, and that awareness may cause you pain. And because you have wonderful parents and family who love you, they will share your pain. Already I see the hurt your parents feel when you behave differently from your playmates.

So why do I tell you this?

Sam, I want you to know that *being* different is not a problem. It's just being different. But *feeling* different is a problem. When you feel different, the feeling can actually change the way you see the world.

Do you remember when we went to Disney World? You were too young and excited to notice, but in many ways I was different from the other people. I couldn't go on many of the rides, I got on the bus differently from everyone else, and I couldn't go swimming with you. Most of the time I felt okay about it. After all, I have been living this way for nearly twenty-five years. But some of the time,

I *felt* different. And those times were pretty sad and embarrassing for me.

The first time I went, about ten years earlier, I'd been thrilled to discover how wheelchair-accessible Disney World is. Every bus had a wheelchair lift. The bus driver had to get out to operate the lift, and everyone on the bus had to wait until I was on. But I was so happy to be able to get around to Adventureland and Tomorrowland, those technical details didn't matter.

When I went with you, the buses were exactly the same, but I wasn't quite so thrilled. I was more conscious of people watching and waiting while I got on. The story I told myself at first was that people were impressed with the technology and happy that I could get around with the rest of them. But that story didn't last long, and the next time I rode the bus, I had a new one. I was convinced that all the people waiting for me to board were hot and tired. They just wanted to get on the bus and didn't want to wait. I was getting on their nerves.

Finally, I got frustrated. Why couldn't it just be easier? I didn't want to hold everyone up while the bus driver went through all the lift preparations. I felt very different. And it was painful.

The bus was the same. The quadriplegia was the same. What changed?

What changed was what I did with my mind.

Your different-ness and my different-ness are just facts. Sometimes what we do with our minds turns those facts into pain, and sometimes we can just treat them as facts, acknowledging them but not feeling them. But the more you *feel* your different-ness, the more lonely you will feel.

Sam, you know what? I no longer worry when your mother says you're perfect. Finally I understand what she means. Your body is not perfect. Neither is your brain. You are different from most other people. But when I look in your eyes and see your sweetness, I can only agree with your mother. In some of the most important ways, you already are perfect.

Love,
Pop

———

PART II

ABOUT YOUR FAMILY

YOUR FATHER AND MY FATHER

Dear Sam,

I began to get a pretty good sense of your father the first time I came to visit him at his house. Before my visit, he asked Debbie and me some detailed questions about my physical needs. As soon as he saw my heavy wheelchair, he began planning how he would build a ramp to his front door. The first day I came to the house, the ramp was ready, built with his own hands.

Later on, when your dad learned about your autism, he said one thing I will never forget. "If Sam can't learn in school," he told me, "I will take a couple of years off work and we will sail around the world. I will teach him everything he needs to know in those two years."

That says everything about your dad's character. To me it says he will do whatever it takes to enable you to have a full life. He is going to make that happen, no matter what.

My father—your pop-pop—loved me just as much as your father loves you. But the way my father expressed himself was much different. His image of fathering came from *his* father, a man who had endured extreme adversity in Russia and was never comfortable in this country. To my father, a dad was someone strict, rigid, and demanding. My grandfather would frequently say to my father, "You should never compliment a child, or he'll get a swelled head." So my parents never paid me a compliment when I was growing up. From time to time I'd hear my mom and dad bragging about me to other people, but I was not meant to hear that praise.

From what your dad has told me, I know that his own father treated him very badly when he was a boy. So your dad has created his own version of what it means to be a father. That's lucky for you, Sam!

The way he talks about the possibility that you and he could sail around the world together? You really could! Ever since he was a boy, your father has had a passion for sailing, and he has crewed on some of the biggest sailboats in the world. I've heard him talk about long-distance ocean races he sailed in from Baltimore to the Bahamas and the Caribbean, and I've seen pictures of him with crews of thirty or forty men. I suspect this is where he gained his self-confidence and a sense of his own skills.

Since you were born, your mom and dad have been able to change their work life. Your dad is a very successful insurance salesman, and Debbie was able to give up her own job to stay home, helping out with the insurance business. That way, each of them can work part-time and spend more time with you.

Whenever I see you playing with your father, I feel like I'm looking at two buddies. It's delightful to watch! Your father brings out his adult self only when needed. Most of the time, it looks like two little boys in a playroom as you go from bumper cars to electric trains to indoor basketball.

And golf.

Your mom tells me that on a recent sunny spring day, shortly after you woke up, your dad came into your room to make plans. "It's a beautiful day, Sam. Let's go out to breakfast, and then we'll go to Target and do some shopping. Then we'll come home and play in the house, and then maybe we can go to Chuck E. Cheese's."

"Oh, Dad," you replied, "it's a nice day! Forget all that stuff. Let's just go play golf."

And that's what you did—just like two little kids.

Watching the closeness between you and your dad, I can't help but think how often there is distance between fathers and sons. My father loved me, too, but he showed it from a distance, by working hard and protecting his family. I want to tell you about my relationship with him and the understanding that we came to before he died.

Your pop-pop was often away from home when I was growing up. Working in his Army-Navy store in Pleasantville, New Jersey, he earned enough money to raise his family in a middle-class suburb and send his children to college. But he worked thirteen-hour days, six days a week. My time with him was both precious and rare.

For a while, I resented that. Then, as I grew, I learned he really didn't like that store very much. But what else could he do to support our household? He worked at something he didn't like for thirty-eight years so that he could care for his family.

When I was young, I thought I saw the rigidity in my father's temperament. As I matured, my vision changed. Now I see that the rigidity was really tenacity. As a young man I was critical of his lack of assertiveness and aggression. Now I think less about those shortcomings and more about his kindness and love for his family.

I always felt physically awkward around my father. I never knew what to do when I greeted him or when I said good-bye. A kiss? A hug? A handshake? He didn't know what to do, either, so we fumbled our way through greetings and partings, pretending that we were both indifferent to this trivial matter.

As adults, whenever my dad and I parted, my mother would wave her hand and say, "Danny, kiss your father!" But we were being manly, and we didn't do that—until one visit several years before my accident, when I was twenty-nine. As we parted, my mother gave her usual advice. But this time, for some reason, she was more insistent when she said, "Kiss your father!" So I did kiss him! And from then on, I kissed him whenever we said good-bye.

At the age of eighty-two, your pop-pop was diagnosed with congestive heart failure. His health deteriorated. It was clear from what the doctor told him that his kidneys as well as his heart were failing and he probably wouldn't get better.

Six months before your pop-pop died, I spent a wonderful month with him in Atlantic City, where his apartment overlooked the beach and the ocean. Since he and I both knew the state of his health, I discussed with him whether he wanted emergency medical attention—to be resuscitated—if he lost consciousness. If he preferred, I said, we could just help him be comfortable in his apartment by the ocean. It was a difficult conversation for both of us, and ultimately he chose comfort over medical attention.

He and I had our last visit the day before he died. It was a very windy day. When I got to the apartment, he was sitting in front of the window, warmed by the sunshine. I pulled my chair next to him. After I rested my arm on his shoulder, we gazed down at the beach together, not saying much.

A strong wind was blowing sand directly into the ocean, erasing all footprints. It seemed that if the wind kept up, all the sand would blow into the sea. The beach was being swept clean. As I watched the beach renew itself, I moved my hand to my father's chest, drawing him closer. Without looking up, he took my hand, kissed my left thumb—the only area on my hand where I have sensation—and gently rubbed his cheek on it.

The next day, his nurse found him in the same place, sitting in his favorite chair in the living room, facing the ocean. He was no longer alive. It was the right way to die and, for him, the right time. I knew that. But for several days after his death, whenever someone asked whether I needed anything, I began to cry. "Yes," I thought, "I need to feel his cheek on my thumb one more time."

As long as I am alive, whenever I am with you, I will be glad to tell you about your pop-pop. He was a small man—small in stature and small in the mark he made on the world. He did not lead any groups or organizations. All he did was marry a woman he adored and raise two children who were capable of love and compassion. He lived and loved. He left the world pretty much as he found it.

Someday, Sam, you will take the measure of your own father. You will see the role he plays in his family's life, in your life, and in your mother's life. You will know the dimensions of his impact on the world. But I know that none of those judgments or measurements matters very much right now. What matters is the way you look at the ocean together.

Love,
Pop

———

AUNT SHARON'S SECRET

Dear Sam,

Recently, Case Western Reserve University in Cleveland created a research program called "The Institute for Research on Unlimited Love," in which much of the focus is on the study of altruistic love. Altruistic love means giving to another simply out of compassion. Not because you think you should. Not because you feel responsible for the other person, or because you wonder what someone else can do for you in the future, or because your charity will help reduce your taxable income. Altruistic love is simply for the sake of the other. The studies at this institute have shown that this kind of love—which is the most pure—is also the most healing.

Did it take an academic institute to teach us that this kind of love is valuable? I think not. We hear about it from the Hebrew Bible. The teachings of Jesus, Muhammad, and the Buddha say the same thing: Giving to others is most precious when it is done quietly and selflessly.

If you'd come along a little sooner, you would also have known my sister, your aunt Sharon. I wish you could have.

She was a great teacher, cut from the same cloth as the greatest teachers in history.

My sister was five years older than I. Like most younger siblings, I idolized her and I was terribly jealous. She was older, pretty, smart, and had lots of friends. I was just a dorky little kid. So, because I was so envious, we fought when we were young. She always won.

I remember the time when she and her friends were babysitting me. I was getting on their nerves and they convinced me to eat a whole box of chocolate-flavored laxatives so I wouldn't annoy them anymore. When the laxatives went to work, sure enough I stopped bothering my sister. But when I later figured out what she'd done, I vowed to get her back for that!

I was about fifteen years old before there finally came a day when I was big enough and strong enough to stand up to her. I'll spare you the details—but anyway, I won the fight, and it turned out to be our last. After that, neither one of us had anything to prove to the other. I was stronger and she was smarter and that was that.

Somewhere along the way, Sharon became my confidante. She knew about the first time I smoked a cigarette, and she knew when I lost my virginity. After I got married, and we realized we were both adults, we grew even closer.

The years passed. Then there came a time when my wife—your grandmother—was diagnosed with cancer. I felt terrified and alone. But I discovered I wasn't. My sister was there.

Many years later, when your grandmother and I decided that our marriage was not going to work, it was

Sharon's opinion and companionship that I valued more than anyone else's.

Then, a couple of years before you were born, my mother called to tell me, "Your sister's been getting a lot of headaches, and I'm worried." I didn't think much about it, because my mother worried about everything. By the third phone call, however, I too was concerned.

Preliminary tests told us that Sharon's headaches were probably caused by a benign growth in her brain. The doctors wanted a biopsy. Her husband, her sons, and I all accompanied her to Columbia University Medical Center in New York. After we'd waited several anxious hours, the doctor came out.

David, Sharon's husband, was standing to my left and her sons were behind me when the doctor reported his finding. "It's a glioblastoma," he said. "It is not curable. She has a life expectancy of eighteen months."

In my breathless shock, I watched David's knees buckle just for a second, as though he'd been punched in the solar plexus.

One hour later, when I visited my still-sleeping sister's bedside and held her hand, I began to write her eulogy.

The doctor was right. Sharon lived about eighteen months, and everyone who knew and loved her watched her slip away day by day.

But I still had more to learn about her.

On the last day of shiva, the traditional mourning period, when people stopped visiting and we began to put the house back the way it was before Sharon died, there was a knock on the door, and in came a man I had never seen before. He had met your aunt Sharon many years before, when she ran a very prosperous business—a franchise that included a temporary employment service and a full-time employment agency.

When Sharon decided to sell the employment agency, this man bought it from her. Afterward, they would occasionally meet for lunch and talk over how the business was going.

As it happened, shortly after the man bought the business, the economy took a turn for the worse. The employment agency was hit very hard. Meanwhile, Sharon's temp agency was flourishing. Because she and this man were still meeting for lunch from time to time, she knew what hardships he was going through. As his anxiety and depression got worse, his marriage suffered and his self-esteem sank lower and lower.

One day, at lunch, the man was in despair. He didn't see how he could keep going, and he was bracing himself to cut his losses and get out of the business.

Just as they were about to leave, Sharon got out the key to her temp agency. She slid it across the table to him. "It's yours," she told him.

No one in our family ever knew anything about it.

"She saved my marriage," this man told me at shiva. "She saved my life."

I wonder what Aunt Sharon would say to you if she could tell you this story herself.

I think I know. I think she would say, "I was blessed because I was able to do that."

That is altruistic love. That's what the great teachers knew, and it's what Sharon showed to that man, to me, and now to you. Giving to others is most precious when it is done quietly and selflessly. She gave him her business because he suffered and she had a way to diminish his suffering. That's all.

Eight hundred people attended her funeral. In my eulogy I told them all about her work for women's rights and Jewish causes, and I asked them to respect her by respecting what she believed in. I told them, in addition, to please take care of the earth, the water, and the air, because, I said, "Sharon lives there now."

Even now, eight years later, I miss her every day. I am grateful for everything she taught me, during her life and even after her death. And I try to practice her lesson of altruistic love every day.

Love,
Pop

———

YOUR GRANDMOTHER SANDY

Dear Sam,

Your grandmother Sandy died before you were born. As you get older, I know you will find out more about her from your mother. But the part your mother doesn't know so well is what happened to Sandy and me during and after our marriage. This is just one little piece of the story, but it's a part that I would like you to know.

At the beginning, our marriage was no different from most. I was a young twenty-three. Sandy was a young nineteen. She was a freshman in college and I was a graduate student in psychology. She was enamored with me. In all my twenty-three years of life, no woman had ever seemed so happy to be with me. And I started to love her within the first ten minutes. Something about her eyes, her smile ... but mostly her gentle soul. All we could see was a future filled with security, happiness, and children—a family!

We married on December 27, 1969, in New York City. Produced, directed, and managed by Sandy's mother, the wedding was a lavish affair that lasted well past midnight. Sandy and I sneaked up to our hotel room hours before it was over.

We were like children, best friends, lovers—even a little

like siblings preparing a new life. In our first apartment, her camp trunk doubled as our coffee table. Despite the lack of fine furniture, she made us a beautiful home.

Our two children came quickly. Then we had a house in the suburbs. And within five years of our marriage vows, the dream was starting to become our reality. Perhaps for the first time in each of our lives, we felt secure, safe, and on top of the world—a story many young married people could tell.

But the stresses began shortly thereafter as my career began to take hold. I was earning a decent income, and I felt like a man for the first time. I felt pride in my work, so I did it a lot—too much.

Then, toward the end of our fifth year of marriage, a few words from a doctor cast a different kind of spell on our lives. "I think the mole is malignant," he said to Sandy.

Learning that she had cancer, we both became frightened, distant, and more insecure than we had ever expected. I think we both felt betrayed—our dreams of safety and certainty were shattered—and we secretly resented each other for that reason. But we had no time for anxiety or anger. We had two children to raise, a home to take care of, a career to maintain, and now chemotherapy to get through.

Time passed, and Sandy healed. But the distance between us grew.

Then, shortly before our tenth wedding anniversary, I was on the thruway, driving out to my uncle's house to pick up a new car—an anniversary surprise. Only later would I learn what had happened. A hundred-pound wheel flew off an oncoming tractor-trailer, bounced across the road, and landed on the roof of my car.

I heard nothing—saw nothing. My neck was broken, the spinal cord severed between my fifth and sixth cervical vertebrae. I could still talk. I had feeling in my face and shoulders. I was alive, and I was a quadriplegic.

If Sandy's cancer took away my security, my disability took away hers.

When any relationship begins to sour, the details are different but the emotions are much the same: betrayal, disappointment, shattered dreams, and deadly silence. How does a young couple like us cope when they lose their footing, security, future, and, perhaps, each other? Like many others, we did it through years of denial, hiding behind parenting responsibilities, and trying to survive one day at a time.

Dependency carries with it resentment. That's inevitable. If people believe they cannot survive without each other, a relationship can be more like a prison than a partnership. As a quadriplegic, I believed I could not survive without Sandy, and she shared that belief. What terrible fear I lived with—that she would leave me, no longer able to endure my dependency—and what a terrible burden she must have lived with.

As it turned out, we were both wrong: I could survive without her.

In June 1989, your grandmother said, "I think I need to move out for the summer." I felt a combination of relief and terror, thinking, "I don't know this person anymore, nor does she know me. I barely know myself!"

Two months later, sitting at a Dunkin' Donuts in Cherry Hill, she told me in words that were stripped of emotion, "I want this to be permanent; I want a divorce." My eyes welled up with tears, but none fell. I wondered, "Who will take care of me now? Who will take care of her?"

She tore away the last illusion of security I felt I had, and I hated her for it.

As in most divorces, our rage against each other became focused on money and material goods. Our lawyers helped us argue, and the system helped us feel ever more furious and more insecure. Finally, one day in court, I heard the sound of a gavel: The judge declared our marriage over. I flashed back to a hotel in New York City twenty years earlier and the sound of a glass breaking under my then-functioning foot at a joyous marriage ceremony. Different sounds, different lifetimes.

The sadness passed, but the rage lasted: "How could she do this to me and our girls? I can't believe she's trying to hurt me! I'll show her." I couldn't even respond when she called me several weeks later to tell me she had been to a neurologist and had a suspicion of multiple sclerosis confirmed. I was too consumed with resentment and fear to even feel the pain of that devastating diagnosis. Finally, we hated each other.

After that, I went through a stage of righteous indignation. I loved complaining about the injustice of the alimony, how hard I had to work, and how much of my income she got. Righteous indignation is like candy when you're starving. It feels good, but it doesn't sustain you very long.

Years passed—maybe three or four—and so did my resentment. I wished Sandy no ill, so I no longer resented the alimony. I just didn't think much about her one way or the other.

Of course, there were fleeting memories, tender and nostalgic moments, but they were uncomfortable and short-lived. Still, I encouraged my daughters to keep in touch with her and maintain their relationship. My daughters needed their mother.

It was Sandy's father who called to tell me that Sandy's multiple sclerosis was getting worse. I could hear the resignation in his voice. I immediately told my daughters. But even as I heard myself asking them to be in contact with her, I knew it was time for me to see her.

Still, several weeks went by. Every day I would promise myself, "Today's the day," and then that day would pass.

When I finally did call, my anxiety was at its peak. What would I find? Would I still feel resentful? Even more frightening, would I feel tender? Would she even know me? Was it too late?

When I heard her voice on the telephone, I could tell immediately that she had difficulty with abstract concepts and short-term memory. All that we could talk about were concrete things: what the girls were doing, what she did every day, how my health was, and so on. We arranged to meet the following week at her apartment. I was fearful, yet oddly excited about seeing her for the first time in many years.

When I arrived, I found Sandy in an apartment

complex that was old and not well kept. It made me feel sad and even guilty to see how she lived. My breathing was shallow, I was so frightened. In fact, I wanted to go home. This was just too difficult!

And then I discovered that there was a physical barrier as well. Sandy's apartment was not wheelchair-accessible.

Unable to enter the building, I called on my cell phone and told her nurse about my dilemma. She asked me to wait on the sidewalk while she helped Sandy get to a patio that was about twenty feet from where I was sitting.

I must have waited five or ten minutes. It seemed like hours. Finally, the storm door opened. I heard the nurse's voice saying, "Move your left foot forward, then move the walker. Now bring your right foot up. That's good, now your left foot, now the walker . . ."

First I saw her hair—long, straight, auburn, almost as it had always been, but without the luster. Then I saw her face. Her features had grown heavy, and her eyes had the darkest rings I had ever seen.

As Sandy tried to maneuver down one step to the patio, she glanced nervously in my direction. I could tell she was trying to maintain some semblance of her dignity while struggling with the walker. I felt awful for her, remembering all of the times she had helped me maintain my dignity.

Before we could exchange a word, the nurse continued: "Turn around and put your right hand behind you, wait until you feel the chair. That's good. Now sit down."

Finally, we could talk. But I had no idea what to say. The physical and emotional distance between us kept me from asking all the questions I truly wanted to ask: What's it like to have MS? Are you depressed? Do you think about your past, and how do you feel when you do? Do you have any energy to fight for your future?

Instead, I asked about her parents, niece, and nephew. We talked about her lifestyle. They were shallow questions—just ways to make contact. I wanted to get closer, to look into her eyes to see if she was still there, and to give her a chance to look into mine. But all I could do was maneuver my head to see her face, twenty feet away, through a black wrought-iron railing.

After promising to meet again at a place that was more accessible, we parted. I turned my wheelchair around and headed toward the van, a sinking feeling in my stomach.

Driving away from the complex, I already knew I would never forget the grief of seeing her that way, with that iron railing between us. So much distance between two kids who had been best friends. It had been easier when I hated her.

I knew the call would come, and it happened two years later. But even expecting that call, I was still shocked, thinking, "Not Sandy." In my heart she was still nineteen years old, and her camp trunk still served as our coffee table.

It was your mother who called me, Sam. She was so stricken. That—and disbelief—was in her voice as she screamed over and over, "Mom is dead."

There was nothing for me to do. So I just lay in bed, barely breathing, not knowing what to think or feel.

Now, many years later, I miss your grandmother. I so wanted her with me when I traveled to Washington to witness your birth. And I have wanted her with me every time I've driven home from your house by myself. I've wanted to share the joy with the only person who could really appreciate it.

And I am happy about that. *Missing* feels like a sad spot in my heart. It feels so much better than when I was angry with her, or worse, when I didn't let myself feel anything about her. *Missing* means I love her.

Love,
Pop

———

PART III

You and Me, Sam

GIVE KINDNESS A CHANCE

Dear Sam,

In the animal kingdom, vulnerability can bring out aggression in other animals. This sometimes happens with humans also. But I have found that, instead, my vulnerability brings out the kindness in people. I see it every day when people hold doors for me, pour cream into my coffee, or help me put on my coat. And I have discovered that when people are kind and helpful, it makes them happy. From my wheelchair perspective, I see the best in people, but sometimes I feel sad because those who appear independent—invulnerable—miss the kindness I see daily. They don't get to see this soft side of others.

Your vulnerability, Sam, along with your radiant smile, will likely attract people who want to be good, who want to help, who feel generous. But what about you? I wonder whether you will be able to expose the soft side of yourself. Often, we try every way possible to avoid showing our vulnerability, which can involve a lot of pretending. But only when you stop pretending you're brave or strong do you allow people to show the kindness that's in them.

Let me tell you a story.

Last month, on a very windy day, coming back from a

lecture I had given to a group in Fort Washington, I began to feel unwell. I was feeling increasing spasms in my legs and back and getting anxious as I anticipated a difficult ride back to my office. Making matters worse, I knew I had to travel two of the most treacherous high-speed roads near Philadelphia—the four-lane Schuylkill Expressway and the six-lane Blue Route.

You've been in my van, so you know how it's been outfitted with everything I need to drive. But you probably don't realize that I often drive more slowly than other people. That's because I have difficulty with body control. I'm especially careful on windy days when the van can be buffeted by sudden gusts. And if I'm having problems with spasms or high blood pressure, I stay way over in the right lane and drive well below the speed limit.

When I'm driving slowly, people behind me tend to get impatient. Someone will speed up alongside me, blow his horn, glare, and show me how long his middle finger can get. (I don't understand why some people are so proud of their middle fingers, but there are many things I don't understand.) Those angry drivers add stress to what is already a stressful driving experience.

On this particular day, I was driving by myself. At first, I drove slowly along back roads. Whenever a car approached, I pulled over and let it pass. But as I neared the Blue Route, I became more frightened. I knew I would be hearing a lot of horns and seeing a lot of fingers.

And then I did something I had never done in twenty-four years of driving my van. I decided to put on my flashers. I drove the Blue Route and the Schuylkill Expressway at thirty-five miles per hour.

Now, guess what happened?

Nothing! No horns and no fingers.

But why?

When I put on my flashers, I was saying to the other drivers, "I have a problem here. I am vulnerable and doing the best I can." And everyone understood. Several times, in my rearview mirror, I saw drivers who wanted to pass. They couldn't get around me because of the stream of passing traffic. But instead of honking or tailgating, they waited, knowing the driver in front of them was in some way weak.

Sometimes situations call for us to act strong and brave even when we don't feel that way. But those are few and far between. More often, the payoff is better if you don't pretend you feel strong when you feel weak or pretend that you are brave when you're scared. I really believe the world might be a safer place if everyone who felt vulnerable wore flashers that said, "I have a problem and I'm doing the best I can."

Love,
Pop

———

COMPASSION WORKS BOTH WAYS

Dear Sam,

In my last letter, I told you how my different-ness draws out people's kindness. When I use an elevator, I need someone to push the buttons. When I'm at a restaurant, I need someone to take the wrapper off my straw. Whenever I drop something on the floor (which is pretty often), I need someone to pick it up. Research shows that doing a kindness for someone else boosts a person's endorphins, the body's natural antidepressants. Your differentness will make people want to help you, too; and helping you will help *them* feel good.

But I think our vulnerability can open hearts—our own and others'—even more powerfully than that. An exchange based on genuine caring can affect people at the very deepest level. If that were not so, I'm not sure I would be alive today.

In intensive care at Jefferson University Hospital, about two weeks after my accident, I truly did not know if I wanted to live—or *could* live—as a quadriplegic. Yes, I still had a marriage and two beautiful children. I might even have a career ahead of me. I was surrounded by people who loved me and told me I was still a worthwhile person. But even if I had a future, I thought I would prefer death to quadriplegia.

When someone breaks his neck, the head must be completely immobilized so the bones can heal. In the old days, doctors would encase the patient in a plaster cast from head to waist, with just the face exposed. The patient looked like a mummy! Today, they use something called a halo vest. Believe me, the halo has nothing to do with angels. It is a metal hoop that surrounds the skull about an eighth of an inch above the scalp. The hoop is bolted into skull bone. (Twenty-five years later, I still have scars on my forehead where the bolts were fastened.) From the halo, stainless-steel rods come straight down, fixed to a fiberglass vest to keep the head from turning.

In the intensive care unit, with my skull bolted in a fixed position, I could not move my head up, down, right, or left. I could only look up at the dimly lit ceiling and listen to the hums and beeps of medical equipment and monitors. IV fluids dripped steadily into my arm. A catheter, implanted in my bladder, drained off urine. The pain in my head was terrible. My only wish was to fall asleep and never wake up.

After a while, I became aware that someone had taken a seat beside my bed. Though I couldn't see her clearly, I assumed it was a nurse—perhaps someone who had treated me earlier, or had just come on duty. A woman's soft voice asked if I was a psychologist. I said I was. She asked if she could talk to me about something that was on her mind. Of course, I said.

It was night and the IC unit was hushed. In a voice scarcely above a whisper, she told me about someone she loved dearly who had left her. With the loss of this love came a sense of aloneness she felt she couldn't bear. Her pain was so intolerable that she was having thoughts of ending her life, and these thoughts frightened her. She couldn't have known I was having some of the same feelings. But because I understood her pain so deeply, I was able to listen with great compassion.

How long did we talk? In my memory the hushed conversation was timeless. It could have been fifteen minutes; it could have been several hours. She told me about her life, her suffering, her loss, and the unbearable pain. She didn't care about my halo vest, my catheter, or my IVs. She didn't care whether I could walk or dance or make love. She didn't even seem to care about my suffering. She just wanted me to help her with her pain. But as I listened to her, for the first time since my accident, I didn't care about my suffering either. I only cared about hers.

She never leaned over my bed, so I never got to see her face. In my mind, in my heart, she has become a magical, mystical voice that entered my life and touched my soul.

That night, after we had talked, I was able to offer her a referral. As she left, I knew that I had been able to help her. And at that moment, I knew I could live as a quadriplegic. From that voice at my bedside I heard that I could still be of value in this world. Everyone else had been trying to convince me that I was still a worthwhile person, but the only way I could really learn that lesson was from someone who asked something of me.

Quite possibly, that evening, she and I saved each other's lives.

Love,
Pop

———

SEEING THE PERSON

Dear Sam,

I can hardly bear to think about it, but I know that someday you are going to overhear someone saying, "He's autistic." At that moment, I fear, you will realize that when some people look at you, they don't see Sam. They see a diagnosis. A problem. A category. Not a person.

In May 1969, when I was twenty-four, a woman named Norma taught me how limiting such labels can be. I was a brand-new psychologist working in the acute psychiatric care ward of a city hospital. Treating Norma was part of my training. I really was not a very good student—I didn't retain information well—and all I knew about psychotherapy was that it lasted fifty minutes. (That's a slight exaggeration—but only slight!)

Norma, on the other hand, had experience; she'd been in and out of psychiatric hospitals for more than thirty-five years. Her chart said "schizophrenic." That was the label she wore when she shuffled into my office for the first time.

Norma came to that first meeting with a sheaf of papers clutched tightly in one hand. Of course, I had to demonstrate right away that I was the knowledgeable professional and I would be able to help her! As soon as I started talking, Norma began ripping the papers. I didn't want to ask her why. I was afraid the question might make her mad. I had the notion that if the patient gets mad, that's bad therapy, and if she doesn't get mad, that's good therapy!

It was a long fifty minutes, but finally we were done. Norma got up from her seat and shuffled toward the door, clutching the shredded paper.

As she got to the door, she turned to me. "You know what?"

"What?"

"You're full of crap." She shook her fist at me. "And I've got the papers to prove it!"

That was the beginning of my relationship with Norma and my first glimpse of the person behind the label. She was right about me. She knew it, and I knew it, and after that, I didn't have to pretend I was something I wasn't. I didn't have to make her believe I knew what I was doing, because both of us knew I had very little idea what I was doing.

And somehow this was okay with Norma. Certainly, her brain worked differently from mine, because she had schizophrenia. But she was not "a schizophrenic." She had told me I could stop pretending, and she had the papers to prove it. Now we could see each other clearly.

Norma never frightened me, though her appearance could sometimes be frightening. She looked very old and wizened. Her mouth was always parched, and she made a constant pill-rolling motion with her thumb and index finger—a common side effect of medication. Also, she could get very agitated at times, to the point that she would need to be restrained. But I wasn't afraid of her. During all the time that Norma and I spent together, I was quite sure there was nothing to fear.

Shortly after your aunt Ali was born, I brought her into my hospital office to introduce my first child to my colleagues. The baby in my arms immediately drew an audience. Though my attention was on Ali, I noticed Norma out of the corner of my eye. She was about thirty feet away, standing in the middle of the public space, making odd gestures as she often did. She seemed pretty lost inside her own mind. But gradually her attention was drawn to the admiring crowd and the object of their attention—the little pink bundle I held in my arms.

Slowly, Norma began to calm down. Over the next several minutes, she made her way toward me. By the time she got there, her eyes looked perfectly clear. She didn't say anything. She just held out her arms, wanting to hold Ali.

I placed my child in her arms and watched her—this scary, disturbed woman—be as sweet and nurturing as anyone could be.

Then she handed the baby back to me, went back into the public space, and got lost again in her mind.

Would I hand my infant daughter over to "a schizophrenic"? Of course not. But I entrusted her to Norma. Norma's illness was a disease of her brain. But her soul was unimpaired.

Sam, I know your mother struggles with having you categorized as "autistic" in school. While she realizes you must be classified that way in order to receive the services you need, she also knows that you are so much more than autistic. She fears that once you have that label, that's all anyone will see.

As I'm watching you grow, your abilities change almost every day. When you were first diagnosed with PDD, your parents and I did all the research we could to find out what was in store for you. We learned that you would have language difficulties. We anticipated that you would first communicate in sign language—as you did for the first three years of your life.

From our research into PDD, your parents and I also knew that it would interfere with your ability to be flexible and to pick up social cues. We were told that you would have trouble with fine motor dexterity, but no problem with gross motor skills. We continue to see that. You still can't put on your coat or open a Ziploc bag. But you've become quite a golf and baseball player.

So the label we learned—PDD—helped tell us some important things about your disability. But it was only a starting point. Now you are talking quite a bit, and we're learning more about who you are. Every day, we make discoveries about your abilities and limitations, your likes and dislikes, what you can tolerate and what you can't.

I know that when other kids are talking, you are not able to go up to them and join in. You sometimes become upset if you can't put on your Spider-Man pajamas right after school. If you open a candy bar and it's already broken, or if you open a box of crayons and they're in the wrong order, you get very frustrated. When you were at Disney

World, you couldn't go on some rides where you had to fasten a seat belt across your lap. Finally your mother understood what the problem was. You were wearing shorts and, to you, the pressure of the seat belt on your legs was terribly painful.

So it's quite true that you have to deal with autism. But autism is not who you are.

A couple of weeks after my accident, I was lying in my hospital bed and I heard my doctor in the hallway saying, "That quad in 301—did he get his medication?" Just a couple of weeks earlier I had been Dr. Gottlieb in some circles. In other circles, Dan. In others, Daddy. And now I was "the quad"?

Well, Sam, over the years I have learned that I am not a quadriplegic. I *have* quadriplegia. You are not autistic. You *have* autism. Because of our labels, some people will be afraid to approach us. Others will be cautious about talking to us or trusting us. With my spinal cord injury and your autism, we look different and act different. But we can also teach people, as Norma taught me, that no matter what happens to our bodies or our minds, our souls remain whole.

Love,
Pop

———

OUR FRUSTRATIONS
AND OUR DESIRES

Dear Sam,

Everyone deals with daily frustration. For you, not having the right-colored pajamas at the right time is deeply frustrating. For me, frustration comes welling up when I drop a piece of paper on the floor and there's no way I can reach it, or when I arrive at a restaurant only to find out there are two steps up to the door.

The root of frustration is desire. As a child, you expect to have your desires satisfied immediately. In many respects, we still wish for instant gratification, even when we're adults. I want what I want when I want it. I want that paper I dropped on the floor, and I want it now! I want the perfect lover and I want my bladder to work and I want my hair back!

The question is not whether we have desires, because we all do. We have the desire for food, for love, for security, and for happiness. We also have the desire to be taken care of.

The big question is, How do we *manage* desire? How do we act on our wants? How do we deal with the frustration we feel when our desires are not satisfied?

Back when your mother and her sister were little girls, they used to make a joke about one of my biggest frustrations. As I maneuvered through the house in my wheelchair, I would occasionally cut a corner too sharply and bump into a wall. When I did, I banged the wall with my fist and yelled out a curse word.

When frustration is unchecked, Sam, it turns to rage, and rage triggers action. I banged my hand on the wall and yelled. You throw tantrums and cry. These are our responses to emotions we experience daily and sometimes find intolerable. The problem is not how you or I feel when these things happen. The problem arises when we can't tolerate those feelings.

I learned from my daughters. Whenever I banged into a wall and vented my rage, Debbie and Ali would laugh. I'd hear them say, "Daddy bumped into a wall again!" After a while, whenever I hit the wall, I'd bang it with my hand, curse, then laugh along with them. "Yup—Daddy hit a wall!"

Maybe it isn't so bad to hit the wall. Maybe the wall is there to teach us a lesson.

Several years ago, on a nice spring day, I was out on the front lawn. No one else was home. Unfortunately, the tire of my wheelchair got stuck in a gopher hole. I revved the motor to drive the wheelchair back and forth, but nothing happened. The chair wouldn't budge.

This happened in the middle of the day, when no neighbors were around and there was no nurse to hear me.

So when I yelled for help, no one came. I yelled even louder, then as loud as I could. Still, no one appeared. Out of sheer frustration, I began banging my hand on the arm of my wheelchair. I banged it so hard, my hand began to bleed. And when I saw that, I yelled again, only more weakly. And then I began to cry at my helplessness.

After I had cried for a while, I just gave up. I didn't yell. I didn't hit my wheelchair anymore. I didn't try racing the engine. I just sat there.

I had hit the wall.

Then—only then—I heard the birds singing. Of course, they had been singing all along, but I had been so obsessed with my desire to get out of that gopher hole, and fighting so hard against my feelings of frustration, and making so much noise in the process, that I'd been unable to hear them. It was perfectly reasonable to want to get rescued, but that desire wasn't going to be satisfied right away. Only when I accepted that, only when I stopped fighting, did I find any peace.

Sam, I watch this process with you over and over again. When things don't go the way you want them to, you rage and you cry. And then you move on. Will your frustration stay this intense for the rest of your life? It's my wish that, as you grow, the process will go more quickly and you can find peace without so much suffering.

Just remember that when you can't find peace any other way, you might run into it when you hit the wall.

Love,
Pop

ANGER AND JUSTICE

Dear Sam,

Wars are fought because of anger gone awry. Relationships are destroyed; marriages dissolve. But there's a way that anger can be productive. Managed appropriately, it can make the world more just. I want you to know that, because you, more than most, will face injustice. And you will have many reasons to be angry.

As you grow, watch your parents carefully as they fight for your welfare. Your parents may face obstacles that are infuriatingly unjust, all because they want to help you get the best quality of life you can possibly have. But as you watch, you will see how they channel their anger into fighting school systems or social service agencies on your behalf. They want justice. Not just for you and themselves, but for many other children with needs like yours. If you fight the right battle, in the right way, the outcome can change not only your life, but also the lives of others.

Sam, you've met a dear friend of mine whom you call Uncle Robbie. He's an attorney. Soon after my accident, he started to ask a lot of questions about what happened.

He learned that a wheel fell off a tractor-trailer that was moving at high speed on the Pennsylvania Turnpike. When the wheel flew off, it crossed the meridian and landed on the roof of my car, crushing the car and breaking my neck.

Who manufactured the wheel? Did the company know it was unsafe? Had accidents like this happened before?

It was Uncle Robbie who said that we should retain a personal–injury lawyer and explore a lawsuit. Your grandmother and I didn't want to. We were too devastated to think in terms of money. That wasn't what we wanted. All we wanted was what we had yesterday! We wanted our suffering to end.

Nevertheless, we gave in. We found a highly respected personal–injury lawyer who filed suit against the tire and rubber company that manufactured the wheel.

The lawsuit was ugly, like most lawsuits. The tire company tried to discredit my story. But over the course of the trial, we found out something that we never would have known. We discovered that the company knew the wheel was defective before they sold it. Knowing the risks, they weighed the dangers against the lucrative contracts. They decided it was financially worthwhile for them to continue manufacturing and selling the wheel. We also learned that there had been many previous lawsuits against this tire and rubber company.

Eventually, we won the lawsuit. As a result of that settlement, I was able to build a comfortable, wheelchair-accessible house in a good neighborhood. It helped me take care of my family as well as myself, and it helped give me the mobility I needed to stay active in my profession. Because of that settlement, I will be able to help you with college and take you to Disney World every now and then. Had I not pursued that lawsuit, my life would not be as good as it is today. I might not even have survived this long, because I would not have been able to buy many of the things I require for my medical needs.

In all those ways, the money has helped. But with my anger, it hasn't helped me at all. No amount of money could make up for my losses. In fact, as I learned more about what the company did and why they did it, I became *more* angry. In the settlement, I was not allowed to name the company publicly—but I wish I could! I wanted my lawsuit to hurt the company enough to call attention to the dangers of selling flawed goods. I wanted them to pay attention to the people who had been killed or injured because of their decisions. I wished that the employees who were responsible would be fired as a result.

You see, Sam, the happiness of "getting revenge" only lasted a moment. That got me thinking about the difference between personal justice and social justice.

When you see two people who are angry with each other, you will often find that their argument is about feelings of injustice on a personal level. If you watch carefully, you will see that when your parents argue with each other, they are probably angry because each one of them feels they've been treated unfairly by the other. Each wants justice. In their minds, if they could just balance the scales, there would be a fair resolution. But the fight to balance the scales of personal justice frequently leads to unhappiness.

Fighting for social justice is a different matter.

My grandmother—your great-great-grandmother—used to say, "If you make the right enemies, you are living a good life." I have argued with doctors who didn't care appropriately for their patients. I filed a formal complaint against a sports stadium that did not provide handicap access mandated by law. I sued an American airline because thousands of disabled passengers had been injured by the people who ran the company, and I knew that thousands more would be injured in the future unless someone fought the airline's practices.

Sam, I know it is human nature to fight for personal justice. And I hope you are able to fight for yourself. But even more, I hope you can turn your anger into the energy to fight for justice for others. If you can, then maybe by the time you have a precious grandchild, he or she will grow up in a more compassionate world.

Love,
Pop

HEALING OUR WOUNDS

Dear Sam,

Shortly after my accident, an occupational therapist introduced me to an anti-gravity device that would help me gain
some use of my arms. The therapist strapped me into slings
counterbalanced with springs, so my arms were literally
weightless. Splints were attached to my hands. In each
hand I held a pencil with the eraser-end pointing down.
Using the feeling I still had in my shoulders to move my
arms and hands and manipulate the erasers, I practiced
turning the pages of a book. As my arms gained strength,
the therapist reduced the springs' pressure so I would
become strong enough to hold them up without the device.
By the end of the week, I was able to turn pages without
any assistance. My wife and the therapist were impressed
by how quickly I'd been able to master this. "Look how
much you've accomplished in one week!"

I felt complete despair.

"Five years ago," I said, "I wrote a three-hundred-fifty-
page doctoral dissertation. And now you want me to be
proud because I can turn a page?"

Sam, I know there will be times when you are hurt.
Even now, when things don't go your way, you feel terrible

emotional pain. But I hope you won't blame yourself or someone else for the pain. And, strange as it sounds, I also hope you will not listen to people who try to talk you out of your pain or show you ways to fix it. Because if you try too hard to fix pain, it only takes longer to heal!

Inevitably, all pain is about longing for yesterday— whatever we had before, whatever used to be. But when pain doesn't go away fast enough, we criticize ourselves for not getting over it, for not being strong enough, or even for being vulnerable in the first place.

Sam, that's not how wounds heal. They don't obey our wishes. Healing takes place in its own way and in its own time.

About a year after that bleak experience of struggling to turn a page, I was back at work. Alone in my office, I attempted to move a printed article from a filing cabinet and put it onto my desk where I could read it. A single staple held together the sheets of paper. As I slid the stapled sheets from the filing cabinet, they started to slither from my grasp. I knew from bad experience that if paper fell to the floor and lay flat, I would have to get someone else to come and pick it up. As the papers started to slide down again, I slowed them with the back of my hand pressing against the filing cabinet. As the papers landed on the floor, they formed a tent, staple-side up, that I knew I could recover. With careful maneuvering, I got my thumb under the staple and gingerly lifted the article up to my desk.

It took about twenty minutes. And as the article finally came to rest faceup on my desk, I felt great pride.

Then I thought back to the previous year. Why did I feel grief then and pride now?

A year before, I was longing for yesterday. This year, I was living in today.

My wound had been healing. Not because I wished it to, not on my timetable, and not by any fancy techniques. I wasn't even aware that I was healing until that moment in my office.

How did the healing come about? The way wounds heal is a miracle. Inevitably, they heal on their own. All we have to do is not let our hungry egos demand that the pain go away on a certain timetable. We need to have faith that the pain will pass. After all, pain is an emotion and no emotion stays forever.

Sam, you will meet a lot of well-meaning people who think they know ways that you can heal more quickly and feel less pain. They may be eager to suggest those ways and may even insist there are things you "should do." They do, indeed, mean well, and most are acting out of genuine caring. But before you take their advice, remember that everything a physical wound needs to heal is already in the body. Oxygen, blood, nutrients are all in there, ready to begin their work. And the moment you are wounded, the healing begins.

Emotional wounds are the same. Sometimes these wounds do not heal because the mind gets all involved and says things like "I should do *this* and I'll feel better," or "Maybe I could do *that* to repair the damage," or "I am hurting because of what another person did, and once they fix it, I will feel better."

All of this mind talk just interferes with the natural healing process. When you feel deeply hurt, you have everything you need *in yourself* to repair the damage. You want compassion, understanding, and nurturing in order to heal. But most of all, you need time.

When I am in a dark tunnel, I want to be with people who love me enough to sit in the darkness with me and not stand outside telling me how to get out. I think that's what we all want.

When you are hurt, be close to people who love you and who can tolerate your pain without passing judgment or giving you advice. As time passes, you will long less for what you had yesterday and experience more of what you have today.

Love,
Pop

———

PART IV

Your Body, Mind, and Spirit

SEX, LIES, AND WHAT IT
MEANS TO BE A MAN

Dear Sam,

My early experiences with girls took place when I was in my teens. And, like most boys of that age, I pretended to know more than I really did, to be more competent and experienced than I was. I couldn't turn to anyone for guidance. Not only that, but I didn't feel I had the option to stop and think about whether I was ready for this activity because there was so much pressure to "be a man." And so I lied. I lied to the girls I was with about my experience, I lied to my male friends about the same thing, and I lied to myself about whether I was ready.

I'm not sure why, but I think it's in the nature of men that we have to pretend we know things. If there's something we don't know, we try to fake it. But that doesn't work well at all, especially when you find someone you love. When you want to find out what feels good and what pleases your partner, it's a lot more helpful to admit ignorance than to pretend to know.

When I was learning about family therapy, I had a great teacher, Carl Whitaker, who felt strongly about the importance of confusion. To him, *knowing* was a lot less important than *searching*. "Confusion is like fertilizer," he said. "It feels like crap when it happens, but nothing grows without it."

Some years later, this advice came back to me when I was a guest expert on a show concerning substance abuse. On the show I was being interviewed by three kids who all asked good, probing questions. One of the questions stumped me, and I said so.

"I don't know," I told the young man. "I'll look it up. Give me a call on Monday."

Afterward, one of the program engineers approached me to say he'd been blown away by that response. "I've never—ever—heard someone say 'I don't know' on this show," he told me.

It was the first time in my life I'd been praised for saying those three words. And it changed something in me. Ever since, I have not hesitated to use them.

Sam, be ignorant. It can be the beginning of something wonderful. When you say to your partner, "I don't know"— or your partner says those words to you—then you can begin to learn about what feels good physically and emotionally. You can learn about sex, love, life, and fear. You can learn about yourself.

When you are with someone for whom you have great affection and respect, ask how you can give and receive the greatest enjoyment. What you discover together is far more than you can learn by yourself. As you learn, you will find yourself attending your partner rather than pretending with her. And when you address her needs with care, love, and patience, you will find your feeling of devotion enhanced multifold. You will know the great happiness of altruistic love.

This kind of love is so pure that you can take great pleasure in your partner's joy and feel great sadness in her suffering. Your most fervent wish is for her happiness. When you love your partner in this boundless way, you can make love when you look into her eyes, share a meal together, or ask her about her day. You can even experience this adoration when you aren't together. You can carry it with you always.

Love,
Pop

———

THE DANGERS OF DESIRE

Dear Sam,

I ended my last letter by telling you that sex is wonderful and you should enjoy it. I mean that. But anything that feels as good as sex also has the potential to get us into trouble. That's true of drugs, falling in love, and even chocolate cake! They feel so good when we taste them that part of our brain wants to have them over and over.

Because sex feels so good, most cultures and religions have set up all sorts of rules and laws to try to control it. There are rules about whom we can have sex with and at what stage in a relationship we can have it. There are rules about whom we can and cannot *think* about having sex with. There are even rules about masturbation!

Generally, people who make these rules are nervous about their own impulses, so they want to control everyone else's. Nevertheless, most would agree that it's probably not a good idea to have sex with whomever you want, whenever you want. And it is certainly a good rule to wear a condom to protect yourself and your partner from sexually transmitted diseases.

Having sex with the wrong partner has gotten many people into great trouble. People have gone to jail. People have been killed. Marriages have been destroyed. Even the president of the United States almost lost his job because he was having sex with the wrong partner.

So why does this happen? There are many reasons. But let's take a look at what sex means and not just how it feels.

Many sex therapists say that for men, sex is a way of getting intimate, while for women, sex is what happens after one feels intimate. I think there's a lot of truth in this distinction. All humans crave intimacy. Among men, there are many who feel unloved and rejected when they don't get enough sex. They get angry and frustrated, or they withdraw, or both. Then their female partners, deprived of closeness and intimacy, feel unloved and not very sexual. (This also happens in gay and lesbian couples. But heterosexual couples, when it comes to sex, are less likely to understand each other's feelings.)

In any sexual relationship, when rejection happens frequently and the craving for intimacy and closeness grows, one or both partners are at risk for seeking it in sex with someone outside of the relationship. This almost always leads to trouble. The odds are very slim that something good is going to result from that outside relationship.

How can we prevent this? We can start by understanding that wishing for something doesn't mean there is a problem that needs to be fixed. It means there is an ache inside. And that simply means we're human. Sam, I

think most of us have more longing for love and closeness than can ever be fulfilled. So the question is not
how we fill that void. The question is: how do we live
with the longing?

Love,
Pop

_____

BRIGHT LIGHT AND STILL WATER

Dear Sam,

Your mind is like a colorful, slightly dangerous neighborhood. Sometimes it's a scary place where you have to be on your guard. Other times, it's a scene of delight. Your mind will try to hold you in the grip of guilt, shame, insecurity, and loneliness. It will remind you of injustice and unhappiness, of death and betrayal, of lies, insults, and embarrassments. Then, perversely, it will surprise you with glimpses of humor, wonder, pleasure, and awe.

You might be tempted to assert your authority over such a complicated and unpredictable mind. Can't you get it to reliably deliver more humor than sadness, more joy than disappointment, more enlightenment than confusion?

Of course, every mind is different. You have already taught me a great deal about the way your mind works, and every day I want to learn more. Now I'd like to tell you some things about mine.

After about thirty years of studying the human mind, I've come to the conclusion that it's like a malfunctioning kidney. Now you may be entertaining some doubts about *my* mind. But stick with me on this.

Every day the kidneys take in about two hundred quarts of blood and filter the blood, separating essential nutrients from wastewater. Every day the mind receives billions of messages ranging from stimulation of the senses to reflection on the past, anticipation of the future, and reaction to emotions. But the mind doesn't do a very good job of deciding which thoughts are nutritious and which ones are waste. Our kidneys filter out a small percentage of waste matter from our blood. Our minds should probably filter out about 90 percent of our thoughts!

Because of our ego's firm conviction that we are the center of the universe, we believe that everything that goes through the mind deserves our attention. So here's a young woman watching a rerun on television when suddenly the thought pops into her mind: "I haven't spoken to my mother in a week! I'll bet she's angry at me."

Then, without a functioning filter, that mind is off and running: "I hate when she gets angry at me. All she does is try to make me feel guilty. She is so demanding and judgmental. Now I'm angry with her. I'll be darned if I will call *her* tonight—she can just wait!"

Or let's say this young woman gets up in the morning and looks in the mirror. Her mind says: "You look awful today! That double chocolate cake you had for dinner must have added five pounds. You have bags under your eyes the size of luggage."

Without a functioning filter, she assumes the way she sees herself is accurate, and when she gets to work, she is self-conscious about her appearance. Her colleague greets her, and she notices he looks away quickly. This only validates her perception that she looks terrible, and she is even more embarrassed!

As I've listened to other people talk about the activities of their minds—and watched the workings of my own—I've seen that this mental activity can ruin a day, interfere with sleep, and greatly diminish our chances of being happy. And all because we just don't have very good filters. Every time we have a thought, we act like a dog when the doorbell rings. We jump up as though it's some important visitor. But it almost never is.

What I've learned about my own mind is that emotions come and go, thoughts come and go. I've got the attention span of a chipmunk on amphetamines. Anxiety is an almost constant companion of my being. It is more or less big, and I am more or less aware of it, from moment to moment.

I have learned I'm at risk for depression. Usually the depressive episodes are mild. I'll have an average of one a year, sometimes two. Sometimes they last a couple of weeks, sometimes a couple of months. And they also come and go.

I've learned that my mind is fluid and changeable and playful; I often find myself creating comedy routines in there. And I have yet to figure out whether I'm getting these laughs because my mind doesn't take me seriously or whether it's because I don't take my mind seriously. Whatever the interaction my mind and I are going to have, I hope we remain friends—but that's probably fluid and changeable also!

Earlier in my life, I tried to control that playfulness because it could get me in trouble. Now I don't worry so much. After all, when you're a sixty-year-old quadriplegic who is also a mental health professional, you can get away with a lot!

Recently, I was invited to address a group at a religious institution on the topic of meditation. As part of my discussion, I decided to do some instruction, so I brought some Tibetan Buddhist bells with me as a way to begin the practice.

I started talking to the group about mindfulness and meditation. And as I do with most discussions, I opened with a story:

"You know, I told a colleague of mine that I was going to lead you in a meditation exercise. And he said to me, 'Man, you need a set of brass bells to do that!'" I held up my Tibetan bells. "'So I ordered a pair on eBay!'"

That's my mind. It doesn't even take mindfulness seriously.

Sam, I would love to know the nature of *your* mind. I would love to feel the world from inside your skin, to see what it looks like through your eyes.

Of course, I've been looking for clues, and you've given me many. I've also learned from people I talk to about PDD and autism.

I had a very well-educated and perceptive man on my radio show, Steven Shur, who has Asperger syndrome, a type of PDD that is similar to high-functioning autism. I asked him to describe what things look like to him. He told me how he perceives both figure and ground features in a way quite different from the way I see them. If someone is sitting in a chair nearby, I see the person first, then the other features nearby, such as the table, chairs, and wallpaper. But in Steve's mind, as he described it, the emphasis is reversed. He picks up patterns in the ground features first—details of the table, chairs, and wallpaper—and only then does he see the figure in the foreground.

Oh, Sam, what I would give to be able to look inside your mind! And I would love for *you* to know its nature. What if you could step outside, look at your inner workings, and say to me, "It's interesting in there"? Someday, perhaps, you will do just that.

I had the opportunity to talk to a wise Buddhist monk who had been practicing meditation for decades. The man had spent his whole life looking at his mind with equanimity. So I asked him to tell me.

"What is your mind like?"

"Sometimes it's noisy," he replied. "Sometimes it's like still water. And sometimes it's like bright light." He paused a moment. "So, it's like that."

How different from the answer I had expected. After all, shouldn't a well-trained Buddhist monk tell me that his mind is always placid, at peace, like an unrippled pool? He looked so outwardly calm and in control. Had he not learned to leash the power of his mind in the same way he controlled his body?

Clearly, he hadn't. He had the honesty and humility to tell me what was more true. His mind was ever changing. He could watch his mind go from still water to bright light and back, but it was not something he could control.

Sam, you're going to meet many people who talk about discipline, control, goals, objectives, and aspirations. You will be told about impulses that need to be regulated, thoughts that should be obliterated, imaginative ideas and visions that need to be restrained. But what I have already learned about your mind fills me with admiration. It's agitated and placid, fast moving and slow, rebellious and compliant; sometimes filled with wild images and sometimes as empty as a cave. The bright light and the still water are both yours, but there's no saying when one will give way to the other. The mind that leaps is the mind that lives.

Love
Pop

YOUR THREE MILLIMETERS

Dear Sam,

An author and sociologist named Frank Abbott has said, "Death is no enemy of life. We would have no idea what life was about if it weren't for death."

About ten years before you were born, I went through a terrible time in my life. And I had a dream that was a revelation.

This was several years after my accident, shortly after your grandmother Sandy had left the marriage. Debbie and Ali had just departed for college. I was home alone. And my beloved sister, who had become my closest confidante, had just been diagnosed with a terminal brain tumor. My heart was in turmoil.

Then I developed a bedsore on my buttocks. This is not unusual for someone who sits in a wheelchair all day, but when it happens, it can be a nightmare. The only treatment for these sores is to stay out of the wheelchair, so what little independence the wheelchair provides gets taken away.

With grief welling up on every side, I visited the doctor. He examined me and said, "It's broken." I said, "I know." He was referring to the skin, but I was talking about my heart. "Too much pressure," he said, meaning my buttocks. "I know," I said, meaning my life.

Then the doctor saw that the wound was moist.

That's an unhealthy sign. "It's weeping," he said, using a medical term.

"I know," I said. But I still wasn't talking about the wound.

Finally he said, "You've got to go to bed for thirty days."

This was my greatest nightmare. Right after the accident, I imagined that everyone would leave me and I would be home alone, confined to bed, with a nurse who was there only because she was being paid. Then, upon the recommendation of this doctor, that's exactly what happened. Displaced from my wheelchair, immobilized, I knew I would not be able to do any of the usual things that sustained me. I couldn't see patients if I couldn't sit up or go into my office. I couldn't get to the radio station for my weekly show. I couldn't drive my van or get around the house by myself. I would have to lie prone, waiting for the wound to heal.

"How do you know it will take thirty days?" I asked.

The doctor explained that skin wounds, if they are in a healthy environment, heal at a rate of one millimeter a day. I wondered about wounds to the heart. How could you measure that healing?

He gave me a brown patch called Deuoderm to cover the wound. I told him I was surprised that the wound would be covered. I thought wounds needed oxygen to heal. Shouldn't the bedsore be exposed to the air?

Yes, he said, wounds do need oxygen to heal. But the

oxygen is in the blood, not in the air. "Everything a wound needs to heal is already in your body," he explained. "We just have to get access to those nutrients and let them work."

Those words stayed with me. If that was the way the body healed, what about the human spirit? Remembering the old prophetic story that tells how infants are born with all the wisdom they need to live, I realized that everything we needed to heal our hearts' wounds might already be in us too.

I went home and went to bed. But the wound didn't heal in thirty days or in forty or fifty. When it finally did close, after about two months, I was elated to get back in my wheelchair. (It made me think—how many people feel overjoyed because they can sit in a wheelchair?) But then it opened up again.

I was devastated. Here came the nightmare all over again. I felt as though my spirit was crushed for good.

Finally, the doctor and I decided that I should have surgery.

One night in the hospital, a friend came to visit me. I told her I didn't think I could go on anymore. What I was feeling went beyond despair. It was a loss of hope—of everything I valued, trusted, and loved. The pain had become simply unbearable.

My friend held my hand and said, "Dan, what you are about is more important than who you are."

. . .

That night, I had a dream. I dreamed that God came to me. This was not the God I believe in, the one you read about in the Bible. It was some other God, and when He spoke, he said, "I'm going to give you a piece of the universe. Your job is to take care of it. Not make it bigger or better—just take care of it. And when I'm ready, I'll take it back, and your life will be over."

I looked at the piece of the universe that God was showing me, and I saw that it was just three millimeters! Was that all? I could feel my ego begin to rail against this indignity. I'm a psychologist! I am an author! I have a radio show! Aren't these things important?

Of course, no matter how much I protested, it wouldn't make any difference. My allotment was still—and would always be—just three millimeters of the entire universe. That was it!

But in this dream I also saw that caring for three millimeters of the universe was an awesome responsibility. A God-given responsibility. Though I had felt I couldn't go on, finally I had to acknowledge that I would have to give back my three millimeters before I was ready. And because, at the time of the dream, I had a wound that was healing in millimeters, I knew that my job was to help heal my three millimeters of the universe.

Sam, part of the reason I'm at peace with my life is that I take care of the part of the universe I'm responsible for. I haven't made it bigger or better. I haven't changed it. But I have cared for it. Writing these letters to you is just one of many ways of tending my three millimeters.

What I wish for you, Sam, is what I wish for

everybody—to get as clear a sense of what your life is about as I got in that dream. Your three millimeters is not much in terms of area. But I hope you will feel the gratitude and joy that I feel, having been given that much to tend.

Love,
Pop

———

THOSE WHO FLOAT

Dear Sam,

Young as you are, I know you already know something about faith. You have faith in your mother's arms. That's a good start. But later on, you'll find it gets more complicated.

Not long ago, I was talking with a woman who got me thinking about what faith really is. She was in her mid-forties, and in therapy she said she felt as if she had been "treading water" her whole life.

"What if you stop?" I asked.

Between you and me, Sam, that is not my most brilliant intervention. But it's a good question. What does happen when you stop treading water? Either you sink or you float.

This woman felt as if she had spent most of her life treading water because she was fighting something inside herself. Some people do that all the time. They fight against fear of death, fear of being "found out," fear of losing their minds, fear of realizing they are not the people they should be, or fear of becoming who they are. But as this woman was thrashing against the water, deep down she knew she would lose the fight.

So when I suggested that she stop treading water, I realized the difference between those who sink and those who float. The very moment you give up struggling with the water, if you're going to float, you have to put your faith in the water—just lie back and let it hold you up.

In my last letter, I told you about my dream and my three millimeters. But something happened to me afterward that I also need to tell you, and it has to do with my own faith. After that dream, something in me went quiet. Not only did I know what my life was about, but also something deep inside me knew my place in the universe. I don't mean my role or my responsibility. I mean, literally, my place.

Outside the window across from my bed, I could see a big tulip tree. I looked at that tree and the foliage around it almost every day. The tulip tree had been there for almost a hundred years, and it would still be there long after I was dead. That felt wonderful. In *Tuesdays with Morrie* there is a story Morrie tells about two waves in the ocean that are talking to each other. The front wave tells the second that it's frightened because it is about to crash into the shore and cease to exist. But the second wave shows no fear. It explains to the first: "You are frightened because you think you are a wave; I am not frightened because I know I am part of the ocean."

Lying in my bed those weeks and months, staring at my tulip tree, I realized that I was simply part of the universe. I could feel my ego, my sense of self, begin to shrink. If a person walked into the room—a nurse, a friend, a patient—I could almost physically feel that person's presence in my chest. It didn't feel like there were two separate beings in the room. It felt like my own being was actually changed by the presence of the other.

I felt the presence of a universal and divine and natural companionship that, in a certain way, I had felt my whole life. When I was a child, that presence was my imaginary playmate. When I was a preadolescent, that presence was a primitive God. Then, from adolescence until my accident, the presence was gone—I couldn't feel anything.

Now it was back, and I knew what it was. It was the kind of companionship I had longed for my whole life. And I realized that I had always had it. I knew then that I would never be alone again.

In Greek mythology, there are two gods who argue over man's soul. The question is, which god will be in charge of it? Unable to settle the question, they decide to divide his soul in half and send each half to a different part of the universe. So, each human is doomed to spend eternity looking for the other half of his or her soul.

In my bed, on the day I had that dream, I discovered the missing part of my soul.

Sam, we wake up and fall back to sleep and wake up again. The things we discover don't stay as vivid or as conscious as they were when we first came to them. But I have faith—whether it is conscious or not, whether it is felt or not—that companionship is there. With that renewed faith, I feel lighter. I can float without kicking.

Love,
Pop

———

THE JOURNEY INSIDE

Dear Sam,

The Bible says that God told Abraham to leave his father's home—to depart from the land that he knew and "go forth." And as he went forward, he should have faith that he would be cared for.

In "going forth," I think Abraham was really setting out to find the missing part of his soul. And a rabbi friend of mine tells me that the literal translation of the words in the Bible *lech le'cha* is "to go inside." So his journey was not just external. It was also a journey into himself.

One day, Sam, you will go forward on your journey. And when you do, you will face great fear and great hope. The journey inside could be the most courageous journey of all.

My own journey was supposed to begin when I was eighteen. That's when I left home for the first time to go away to college. All through high school I had struggled with a learning disability. Now that I was alone, that disability loomed as an obstacle. In addition, I was frightened and depressed. To make matters worse, my roomate was anti-Semitic, and I was afraid of him. That made me feel even more alone.

With all these burdens, I failed most of my courses. I wasn't allowed to register for the second semester. This was in the middle of the Vietnam War, a war that frightened me, as well as a war I didn't believe in—and I knew if I couldn't stay in college, I would probably be drafted. If I couldn't make the grades to keep me in college, I would end up over in Vietnam fighting that war.

I did what I had always done when I felt scared and alone. I called my mother.

For the first time she said, "I can't help you from here. You have to do it on your own."

That's the moment I identify as the preface to my journey.

I insisted on meeting with the president of the university, and with a lot of persistence I finally got to see him. I told him my story and asked him for another chance. He agreed to let me stay one more semester. Something about that moment changed me too.

As it turned out, though, the expectations of the school were beyond me. I wound up going, the next year, to the only full-time night school in the region, which happened to be at a Catholic university. It turned out to be one of the most important years of my life. I lived alone. I made no friends. But I developed some academic skills, surprised myself with my resilience, and discovered my ability to tolerate solitude. My real journey began there— in solitude.

Of course, I didn't begin there by choice. And when the time comes for you to begin your journey, I hope you are in a different position. I hope you can begin your journey when you're ready, and during that journey, I hope you have some sort of safety net. But I also hope you see that solitude lets us learn more about who we are.

I have prominently displayed in my office a poem by an anonymous author. It's called "Come to the Edge":

"COME TO THE EDGE!"
"No, we cannot . . . we are afraid."
"COME TO THE EDGE!"
"No, we cannot . . . we will fall."
"COME TO THE EDGE!"
And they came and he pushed them,
and they flew!

When I read that now, I am reminded of another moment in my life when I found myself in uncharted territory. Immediately after my accident, everyone looked at me differently—even my parents. Until then, I had always felt that they were ahead of me on life's path, and that almost anywhere I went, they had been there before me. But now I was beginning an experience that they had never had before, one they could hardly imagine. And the moment they looked at me, I knew I was on this path by myself. Wherever I would go from that moment on, it would be a place no one had gone before me. It was terribly sad, terribly frightening, and freeing at the same time.

• • •

Sam, if we are to become the people we were meant to be, we must take this journey. Like Abraham, as we embark we must have faith that we will be okay on the other side.

When you hit late adolescence, you will leave your parents' home—if not literally, certainly metaphorically. You will have to go forth—and go within—to create your own life.

Take with you the wisdom you have acquired from your parents, your grandparents, and your teachers. But remember, their wisdom is not necessarily your truth. Like Abraham, you must go forward in faith, and you must always be attentive to the quiet voice of your heart.

Love,
Pop

———

PART V

What's Ahead for You

LOSING YOUR BINKY

Dear Sam,

Happy fourth birthday!

I want to congratulate you on an important year for your growth and development. Some of your repetitive behaviors have improved. Your speech is better. I can see that you have begun to develop an internal moral compass, observing what is right and what is wrong with people's behavior. And your mother told me that, this year, in your preschool play, you were finally able to sing with the rest of the children! But the news is not all good. We are still concerned about your rigid behaviors and how upset you get in the face of change.

Sam, change is difficult for all of us. The older we get, the more change we face. All change involves loss, and whenever we lose something, we ache to have it back. Everything I have lost in my life—big things and little things—I've wanted back at first.

So because we know that all change is loss and all loss is change, your mom and dad worried about how you would react when it was time to give up your beloved pacifier— your "binky."

For several months before your birthday, your parents

told you that four-year-olds don't use binkies. In the final weeks, I could see you were both excited and scared about giving it up. On the big day, your mother took you toy shopping and traded in your binky for a toy. When you got home, you cried. "I don't want to be four anymore!" you wailed. "I want to be three!"

Many years ago a British psychoanalyst named D. W. Winnicott coined the term "transitional object" to describe how you move from dependence on your parents to independence. Things like baby blankets and pacifiers represent a parent's touch and help you manage anxiety and insecurity during this transition.

Remember how you cried that first night?

Now that you no longer have your binky, you have nothing to protect you from your anxiety. That's why transitions are hard. Those transitional objects give us the illusion of security. When they are gone, we are left with the insecurity that's been there all along.

Sam, almost everything we become attached to we'll eventually lose: our possessions, our loved ones, and even our youth and health. Yes, each loss is a blow. But it's also an opportunity. There's an old Sufi saying: "When the heart weeps for what it's lost, the soul rejoices for what it's gained."

As much as anyone who loves you would like to rescue you from your pain and give the binky right back to you, that wouldn't be a good idea. Each stage of growth involves loss. Without it, you can't have the gain.

So when you feel the pain of loss, please don't grab at something to take away the pain. Just have faith that pain, like everything else, is transitional. Through it, you will learn about your ability to deal with adversity. You will learn about how you manage stress. You will feel pride. On the other side of the pain, you will learn something about who you are.

A friend of mine recently told me she had so many difficulties in her life that she felt like she was living in a nightmare and didn't know what to do. I told her to find the bus station and wait for the bus! She looked at me like I was crazy. I explained that all emotions are temporary, and we can wait for them to pass as though we were waiting for a bus. We can wait with frustration, anger, or feelings of victimhood, but that won't make the bus come any faster. We could wait with patience and relaxation, but that wouldn't make the bus come faster either! Like all buses, it comes when it comes. We just have to have faith that it's coming.

Everything is temporary—good feelings, bad feelings, binkies, grief. But maybe I don't need to tell you that. When I visited you last week, just one week after your birthday, you didn't bring up missing your binky one single time. And you seemed quite proud to be four instead of three.

Love,
Pop

THINGS TO REMEMBER
ABOUT BULLIES

Dear Sam,

Because of your autism and because you are very small, you are at high risk of being bullied. My guess is that you're going to meet up with bullies at school. You're also going to meet them later on. Learning to deal with them now will help you then.

There are things I want to tell you about recognizing bullies. But the most important thing is that *dealing* with bullying at this stage is something you and your parents need to do together. So this letter is for your mom and dad as well as you.

You first.

It might help you to know a little bit about the kids who do the bullying. People who feel good about themselves and their lives don't try to dominate other people the way bullies do. Psychologists say that it's *hurt* people who are most likely to try hurting others, and I certainly think that's true with bullies. When they try to push other people around, they are really trying to make themselves feel more secure. Of course that doesn't work. But they keep pushing—harder and harder.

When you encounter one, I'll bet your first reaction will be fear. Then you will either feel ashamed of yourself or get angry. But when you're dealing with a bully, fighting back rarely helps and often makes things worse.

A Buddhist teacher once said that a poisonous snake is only poisonous when you walk toward it. A bully is like that poisonous snake. When you walk away from a bully, you are not being a coward, you are being smart.

Next, you have to tell someone about how you've been bullied. A teacher or principal might help, but it's really your parents who need to know first. They realize that bullying can't be ignored, and they will make sure that other adults know that as well.

This is the part of the letter that's for your parents. If you're being bullied, what should they do?

Well, your aunt Ali taught me what not to do.

When Debbie and Ali were in school, a bully on the bus gave them a terrible time. He teased viciously, swore, and physically intimidated them. When Ali told me about it, right away I called both the bus company and the school principal and insisted they do something about it.

The next day, when Ali came home from school, she was angry with me. Because of my intervention, the principal had talked to my daughters. He meant well, but that was beside the point. From what the principal said, Ali knew at once that I'd told him everything. Then Ali and Debbie had been singled out, which embarrassed them. That wasn't what she and Debbie had wanted when they talked to me. I was supposed to listen to them. Then, together, we were supposed to figure out what had to be done.

As parents, we're outraged when bullies make our children miserable. But we have to understand that it's not about us and our outrage; it's about our children and their needs. We have to put aside our own anger and anxiety to help in the way that's best for them. If a child is in danger, of course we need to act at once. But short of that, we need to listen.

Years after that school bus incident, a patient told me about a bullying episode from her childhood that had left her deeply troubled. But the most troubling aspect was not what had happened to her. It was the way it had left her mistrustful of her own parents.

When this woman was twelve years old, walking home from school by herself, she was approached by a group of older boys who intimidated her, poked her, and touched her inappropriately. She managed to get away from them. When she got home, her mother was not there, but her father saw at once how upset she was, and she told him what had happened. She also identified one of the bullies as a boy in the neighborhood.

Enraged, her father ran out of the house to the home of the boy she had named and forced his way in, past the boy's parents and upstairs to the boy's room. He started beating the boy, and he wouldn't stop until the police intervened.

When the father rushed out of the house to beat up the boy, he had left his frightened daughter alone. He ended up in the police station, of course. The story got around school.

His daughter was humiliated. But the worst part was that the battle became all about him and not about her.

Telling me this, the woman realized that her own trauma got worse instead of better because of what her father did. After that scene, she didn't talk to either parent when she was upset.

Sam, I'm quite sure your mom or dad would never do anything like that. But the impulse is there. They have to deal with their own rage in a way that lets them see what is best for you.

So what would I advise them to do?

Let me tell you what my own mother did when I was bullied by a teacher during my junior year in high school. The teacher had given me a C when I thought I deserved a B, and I said so. I met with him, made my case, and thought I must have been convincing, because he changed my C to a B.

Six weeks later, I was called to the principal's office and accused of changing the grade on my report card. I told the principal what had happened. The principal called in the teacher, who denied he had changed the grade. When I got home—because I was in danger of being suspended—I told my mother the whole story.

When I asked if she would help me, she agreed. The next day, she came into the school loaded for bear. The teacher backed down. The principal apologized. My grade was restored to a B.

And I was happy my mom did what she did. She fought

for me, but first she listened. I asked for help, and she helped me. The battle wasn't about her, it was about me. It was about taking care of her son.

So, Sam, whenever you get bullied, please make sure your parents read this letter before they do anything about it. I want them to be able to act for you rather than for themselves. And I want you to trust that when you need to talk, they will listen.

Love,
Pop

TAKING CARE OF YOUR PARENTS

Dear Sam,

As I watch your parents take care of you and see how worried they sometimes get, I wish I could do more to ease their minds. But then I think—well, they have you! And while they're taking care of you, you're also taking care of them.

I was reminded of this just the other day. You were in a swimming pool with your mother playing a game you usually play with your dad. You take a dive, then stay underwater for a while. Usually, it's your dad who grabs you and pulls you up. But as I watched you play this game with your mother, I observed that she pulled you up more quickly than you wanted. (I know why, of course. She worries more!)

You were getting frustrated.

One of those times, after she pulled you up too quickly, you stopped the game. You held her face in your hands and said, "It's okay, Mommy, you don't have to worry, I won't get hurt."

Sam, I love the way you take care of your parents. That's a wonderful and natural part of family life. But carrying your parents' burdens is not your job. I have always said that when parents don't do *their own* work—when they don't fix their own problems, fulfill their own desires, live out their own lives—they're really mortgaging their souls. And when they mortgage their souls, their children wind up paying the interest.

Many parents don't realize how much their children *do* worry about them. Over the last several years I have spoken with hundreds of schoolchildren about stress. Most of them feel their parents endure a huge amount of it. The parents may think they can keep stress secret, but it rarely works that way, and the effect on children can be profound. When parents worry about money, their children are likely to long for it, not because they're growing up money-hungry but because it might be a way to family peace. When parents focus too much on achievement and accomplishment, their children are likely to put great pressure on themselves to excel—even in activities that used to be just for fun, such as neighborhood sports—in part so their parents will have one less thing to worry about.

I meet many children who feel like they have to make sure they don't add to their parents' stress. Yet many of them are driving themselves almost as hard as their parents. And whenever these kids have a problem or get upset, they keep their feelings to themselves. That's another way of protecting their parents.

So, what can you do for your parents? What can they do for you?

Sam, I know your mother won't stop worrying. She worries because she loves you, she worries because you are more vulnerable than most children, and she worries because it's in her genes! Your parents cannot help but worry about you—that's one of the ways we care for our children. But the best way you can take care of them is not by taking on their burdens; it's by never letting them forget the value of play, the importance of just hanging out together.

See, if children could hang out with their parents, I think they would be getting more of the kind of parenting they really need.

Many years ago I saw a young man in consultation. He was about twenty-three years old and was having difficulty with his life. He had tried college and dropped out, tried various jobs and quit, and he could not find happiness or success. In our session, I asked him about his relationship with his parents. He explained that his parents had divorced when he was about twelve, and he divided his time between them. But his father was, and still is, his best friend.

He recalled with great warmth the early years of his childhood. But then he told me how worrying had become a constant in his dad's life. At first, his dad always worried about his marriage. As the marriage ended, he worried more and more about his career. Now all he seemed to do was worry about his son and his future. The young man told me that he still felt very loving and close to his dad, but clearly the worry was clouding their lives.

The next time, I met with the young man *and* his father. When his father asked what he could do, I was prepared.

"Your son is seeing his future through your eyes," I said, "and it doesn't look pretty. All he sees is worry and stress. He sees no pleasure in adulthood. That might be part of the reason he hasn't been doing adulthood very well so far."

The father thought quietly for a moment, then asked if he should be in therapy himself. I told him I thought therapy might be helpful, but the important thing was to change his life. It would be an act of love for his son.

You see, Sam, parents never stop being parents and we always see our future through their eyes. We can take care of them by being open and honest and reminding them about the importance of joy. And sometimes the best way they can take care of us is by taking care of themselves!

The beauty of being in a family is being in a family. When I think back to the easiest moments in my own childhood, they were the times when we all sat together in the living room and watched *Bat Masterson*. No one said a word during the show, and when the commercials came on, we talked about the snack, the show, or one another. It was my favorite family time.

When your mom and Aunt Ali were growing up, we had a jar of gumballs that we kept in the kitchen. You've been in this kitchen—you know how big it is—and it's a great hangout room! The chairs you see today are the same ones we had back then, comfortable armchairs with casters on the feet.

When dinner was over, there was a moment of anticipation while Debbie and Ali waited for the magic words. I would glance at the jar. Then I'd yell, "Gumball time!" and off we'd go. I would race to the bowl and pull it onto my lap. Ali would shoot across the floor in her rolling chair and seize the back of my wheelchair. Debbie would grab the back of Ali's chair and I'd race off with the two of them rolling along behind me, hanging on for dear life. We rode around the house as fast as we could while their mom hollered at all of us, "Someone is going to get hurt! Three children I have to deal with!"

But no one ever got hurt at gumball time.

How can you take care of your parents? How can they take care of you? I think you already know how.

Love,
Pop

————

ROAD MAPS

Dear Sam,

Once, a man came home late one night to find he was locked out of his house. His neighbor saw him searching for his keys under the streetlight and joined him in his search. Soon several other neighbors joined in, everyone trying to help their neighbor find his keys.

After a while, one of them asked where he'd last seen the keys.

"Near the front door."

The neighbor was puzzled. "Then why are you looking all the way down here by the streetlight?"

"Because the light is better!"

Sam, this parable comes to mind as I'm thinking about the road maps that we use to guide us in our lives. Often when we look for answers, we automatically go where the light is better. But sometimes we need to go where it's dark.

A personal road map is a philosophy of life, which includes a philosophy about people. Generally this philosophy gets handed down directly from our parents, then modified over the years with beliefs absorbed from our family, community, or religion and opinions derived from our own experience. One road map might say, "The world is *dangerous*; eat or be eaten." Another might show a different picture: "People are basically good and trustworthy and the more people you have in your life the better off you will be." Other people's road maps might suggest that certain *kinds* of people cannot be trusted, so your circle of friends should only include people who are like you.

Just think how these maps guide people in different ways through the world. Compare one person's map that says, "Life is a difficult series of problems to be resolved with little joy," with another that says, "Life is a treasure to be grateful for." With such contrasting views, even if those two people lead similar lives, they will experience the events of their lives quite differently.

The road map also includes a philosophy of ourselves. Am I basically a good person, or am I somehow not quite good enough? Is goodness inside of me or is it something I have to work hard to achieve? Am I fragile and easily wounded? If I run into a serious problem, will I break, or am I resilient? Am I needy, or lovable, or manipulative?

Our answers to these questions shape the kind of map we carry in our psychological "pockets." They form our own guide to how the world works, how people are, who we are, and what we will and won't get in life.

Sam, what will be your road map?

Let me tell you about mine.

When I was young, my mother saw the world as a

dangerous place. If I was going to survive in this world, I needed to be aware of the dangers and be highly vigilant. My father shared this view, though to a lesser extent.

Both my parents were the children of Russian immigrants who had endured great adversity under the czar. So it's not surprising they saw the world as a place where they had to stay on guard. When my grandparents moved to America around the turn of the century only to find pervasive anti-Semitism, their fear and mistrust of the world were confirmed and handed down to my parents. So, when my parents grew up, not only did they face anti-Semitism, but also they endured a crushing economic depression! So their lives, too, were difficult—which reinforced the philosophy that life is difficult and you should only trust your own kind. This is the road map they handed me.

But this view just didn't ring true to me. What I saw didn't seem to be the same as what they were seeing. I liked people of all kinds. And since my parents were effective providers and caretakers, my world felt safe.

As a result, I felt different from my family. Yet I was never confident in my own perceptions, because my family always told me that my views were wrong! Often when my mother and I talked about people and I commented on how nice they were, my mother would "clarify" my perception by saying, "Wait till you get to know them!"

Some early encounters with my grandmother contributed to the feeling that I was not just wrong in my views, but downright bad. As a little boy of five or six, I was very playful, even rambunctious. My Russian grandmother—

who had been viciously persecuted by the czar's soldiers—would hit me in the legs with her crutch and call me "a little Cossack!" I never really knew what she meant, but I figured it was something bad. If she was a grown-up and she thought I was a really bad boy, maybe I was.

So I went through the first years of my life not knowing for sure whether I was open and caring or simply naïve, even stupid. And making the dilemma even worse, there seemed to be a strong possibility that I was actually a bad kid. That was my road map—not clear about who I was, feeling that the ground underneath me was not stable, thinking I might be totally in the wrong. Unlike the man in the parable, I didn't even have a light to search by.

Now, you might think my road map would have become clear when I reached adulthood. But it really didn't change very much until I had my accident. Afterward, for some reason I couldn't understand, people kept coming to me—friends, family, patients, even strangers—wanting to sit with me and tell me about their lives and hear about mine.

Some of them said that even though I was thirty-three years old, it felt as if they were sitting with an old man. And I felt that way too. Not only was my neck shattered, so was my unclear road map. I was searching in the dark for my truth about who I was and what it meant to be human.

Through college and beyond, I had begun to see that my mother's views were not right for me. But later, after my accident, I was able to see that Mom's views were based on anxiety and insecurity and maybe even a low-grade depression. Over the next couple of decades, my road map evolved on its own.

Today, I can describe my map pretty clearly, and it looks something like this: Whether my perceptions of the world are right or wrong doesn't really matter. Like all humans, what I'm looking for is a kind of internal security—a sense of a life well lived. I'm looking for intimacy, community, and love. And at this moment in my life, that's what I have.

Sam, the only way to find a new road map is to be willing to search in the darkness. In my case, the search wasn't voluntary. It came about because of what happened to me. But however it happens, I believe that you need to find a map that's your own. Not necessarily the road map you grew up with, or the one that was handed to you, but another map entirely.

So, Sam, how will your road map come into your hands?

Right now, I see you clutching tightly the one you already have. Most kids do—and this is even more true of children who have autism. You need things to be the way you need them. For you, the first step into the darkness might be the day you come home from school and don't put on your pajamas. Or the first time you allow your crayons to be out of order. But however you take that first step, it's my hope that, over the years, you will become more secure within yourself and not clutch your road map quite so tightly. Clutching anything, after a time, becomes exhausting.

When you let go, what will you find to take its place? When I imagine your road map coming into your hands, I think of a story I heard about a teacher and a young boy. This boy went to study the Bible and found it very difficult.

Seeing the trouble the boy was having, the teacher held up a single bright red apple and said, "This apple is all that's in the Bible. You can have it if you want!" Immediately, the boy jumped up to grasp the apple. He couldn't reach it, so he jumped again—missed again—and jumped even higher.

After a lot of frenzied jumping, he finally sat down, exhausted. As he did so, his hands fell open, palms facing the sky. And the teacher dropped the apple into his open hand.

It's my wish, Sam, that one day you will be able to face your life with palms open to the sky. And I'm confident that the road map you need will come into your hands.

Love,
Pop

WHAT DOES HAPPINESS MEAN?

Dear Sam,

A number of years from now, you may be sitting among classmates and friends as you listen to a commencement speaker tell you about your place in the world and the opportunities that lie ahead. I wonder what the world will be like then. I wonder about the person you will be. And I wonder what you will hear from that speaker.

But I might as well tell you what I would say.

Not long ago, I was asked to give a speech to graduating honor students at Lincoln University. The administrators who invited me wanted me to talk about adult responsibilities and the pathways to success.

I began my speech by saying that success and adult responsibilities can be harmful to your health. As I spoke, I was thinking of a conversation I'd had some weeks earlier with a hundred high-achieving, college-bound seniors in a very upscale suburban high school. I had asked those students why they worked so hard. Almost unanimously, they agreed that their hard work was to help them get into the best possible colleges.

I asked, "Why?"

They replied, "So we can be happy."

"Let's talk about that," I said. "What does it mean to be happy?"

One kid declared, "If I have a million dollars in the bank, I'll be happy." Another announced, "If I'm number one in my chosen profession, I'll be happy. But I won't settle for number two."

The discussion continued with comments in a similar vein. All agreed that money, success, and achievement would make them happy. Not one of these seventeen- and eighteen-year-old kids talked about love, children, relationships, marriage, community, or friends. Which made me wonder: When your résumé is perfect, how does your soul feel?

I suspect I know why these children strive for the overflowing bank account and the perfect résumé. As humans, we grasp at things that make us feel more secure. We go from our mothers' breasts to pacifiers, from small toys to big toys, from cars to houses and vacation homes. Needing security, we grasp at sex, wealth, food, power, drugs. I know it's always been this way.

But the grasping seems worse than it has ever been. It's more aggressive and desperate, less reflective, more selfish. And we are listening to leaders and teachers who tell us that greed is good.

What are we really hungry for? Security and happiness, yes. But the kind of security we yearn for is a *feeling* of security that cannot be attained by acquisition. If we can buy big houses and powerful cars, we may be able to achieve the illusion of security, but it is still just an illusion. If we can do well at school or work, we may get a sense of accomplishment, but there will always be something more to accomplish—happiness will always be around the next corner.

Real security only comes when we are comfortable with who we are (and the feeling is enhanced when we are in a relationship where there is mutual love and understanding). Real happiness is a byproduct of a life well lived.

These were some of my thoughts as I addressed the parents who had come to see their children graduate from college. I told them they had done their job, they had paid their dues, and their reward—their children—sat in front of them.

"Your job now," I said to the parents, "is to enjoy the benefits, tolerate your children's failures, have faith in their resilience, and never, ever offer advice without being asked for it." (That brought a round of applause from their children.)

Then I turned to the students and said, "This is the time when the commencement speaker tells you what to do. So I'm going to tell you. Find someone you love, and feel that love in every pore of your body. Love that person even more tomorrow. And then the next day, love one additional person; and every day after that, increase the number of people you love."

I told them the longer the list of people they love fully, the happier they will be. That, I said, is true success. That is an essential adult responsibility.

Sam, I don't know if I'll be around for your commencement. Perhaps you won't even have a conventional graduation ceremony when you make the transition from your school and classrooms into the working world of adults. But however your résumé measures your success, I hope you will remember what your soul needs. Not wealth, prestige, and possessions, but the adult responsibility to love someone every day a little more than you did the day before.

Love,
Pop

FIG LEAVES

Dear Sam,

One of the first stories in the Bible is about a man and a woman wandering around in a fabulous place called Eden. This is the best garden you could ever imagine, and as the two people spend time there, they get to know each another. All of a sudden, they look down and realize they are naked!

This story takes place in the days before department stores, so they can't hop in the car and drive to the nearest mall. Instead, they rush into the forest and grab some fig leaves to cover their "private parts."

How did they know they should be embarrassed? What made them realize certain parts were "private"? I don't know. But I do know this: What they were feeling was shame—a very natural and common emotion. And whoever wrote the story understood that shame is about exposure.

But in my view, that's not the end of the story. Let me tell you why.

As you grow up, you will begin to compare yourself to other people. We all do. But the comparison rarely works in our favor. In fact, whenever we compare ourselves to others, we usually wind up looking bad. We tell ourselves that other people are smarter, more competent, better looking, and so on. And what do we feel? Shame. We feel shame because we don't think we are the people we think we should be.

Many mental health professionals would say that shame is the most painful emotion there is. They might be right. Often, people who feel shame wind up hating the people who trigger this emotion. So much violence happens because people have been "dissed"—disrespected—but it's really not about disrespect. What it really means is that someone said something or looked at you in a way that made you feel shame. Someone exposed you, and exposure makes us feel isolated.

When I was young, I was for my age small, and the bigger kids used to bully me. One day on the playground, several of them pulled my pants down. The shame was not just that my pants were down, but that others saw me that way and I felt alone.

That was decades ago, but shame never goes away. Even at my age. Sometimes I am ashamed of my big belly or the fact that I need so much help. But believe it or not, Sam, because exposure causes shame, exposure can heal it too. And when that happens, it is a very freeing experience.

One evening, I was sitting in my office having a session with a seventeen-year-old girl. She was complaining about her physical appearance. She hated the way she looked.

Hearing her describe herself, I felt sad because, like most girls, she was beautiful. But her sense of shame made it impossible for her to see that. She measured her appearance against other girls in her class or young models she saw in magazines, and when she made these comparisons, she didn't like herself.

How could I help her? I knew that reassurance would be a waste of time and maybe even harmful. If I made positive comments about her looks, as most people probably did, she would feel that I didn't understand her suffering and didn't care to. I knew that from all the times people had tried to reassure me. It just made me feel even worse about myself, and misunderstood on top of that. So there I sat in silence for a moment, just feeling her shame and my sadness for her.

To finish this story, I have to tell you something about a very different kind of body—my own. Because my bladder doesn't work, I wear a catheter that drains into a bag strapped to my leg. And occasionally things go wrong with the catheter.

As I was listening to this young girl talk about feeling ugly and unacceptable, I glanced down at my lap and saw that my catheter had leaked. My pants were soaked with urine. I looked up at her, overwhelmed with my own shame. And she looked down and saw my wet pants.

I can't imagine a greater embarrassment. If I had been in the presence of anyone else—a boy, a man, even a mature woman—I might have felt less humiliated. But my embarrassment in front of this teenage girl was so intense that I wanted to hide somewhere and cry.

Seeing my suffering, she got up from her chair, came over to me, and held me. I was so moved, I just let her care for me as I relaxed.

Of course, I had to end the session early. But before I did, we talked about our mutual shame and how painful it is—how some of it is necessary, but some of it isn't. So there we were, Sam, just two humans feeling the same painful feeling at the same time. Before this happened, she had felt isolated in her "unacceptable" body, and at the moment I saw my pants, I had felt isolated too. We looked into each other's eyes and saw each other at our most vulnerable. And in that instant, the shame went away from both of us, because we knew we were understood.

Sam, most of the time we work very hard to show one another our best sides. We're careful with clothes, makeup, and how we present ourselves. We cover up what we consider shameful, showing other people only part of who we are.

In that session, this young woman and I had our darkest sides, our shameful sides, exposed to view. And still we embraced. We showed mutual understanding and respect for each other, based on who we were, not just the parts we wanted others to see. Now that's intimacy.

In every one of my speeches, I say, "The hunger to be known exceeds the hunger to be loved." After that session, we knew each other, and ourselves, much better. And with our exposure, both of us began to heal.

So why does the story of Adam and Eve seem so unfinished? The Bible doesn't tell us exactly what happened next. But we can guess. Adam and Eve knew what was behind the fig leaves—they'd already seen each other without them—and they knew the shame and confusion they had shared. When two people see each other without their fig leaves, the chances of intimacy are vastly increased.

It seems quite likely—to finish the story—that Adam and Eve fell in love.

There's another story about shame that I'd like to revise. *The Emperor's New Clothes* needs a new ending. In this book, an entire village convinces the emperor that he is wearing a beautiful suit of clothes when he is really naked. In the original story he parades through the village showing off his "new clothes" and everyone claps while, secretly, they're laughing at him. They assume he'd be ashamed if he knew.

But that's the part I would change. In my version, the emperor knows he is naked, and he still feels pride.

Sam, your pants-wetting days are over, so it's not likely you will experience that particular shame in the near future. Nonetheless, I know it will visit you in other ways. So I hope that when you do feel shame, you will seek out someone who loves and accepts you for who you are. In the intimacy that exposure brings, there's an amazing opportunity: a chance of being loved for who you really are.

Love,
Pop

PART VI

Your Place in the World

THE SMELL OF PEACE

Dear Sam,

Prejudice and hatred have probably been around since we lived in caves. And I'm sure they will not disappear during your lifetime. But perhaps we'll be better off if we learn more about where they come from. At least that is a beginning.

Often, prejudice begins with a feeling that we ourselves are insecure. In order to feel better, we are drawn to people who look, think, or act like we do. That generally works just fine—unless we still feel insecure. Then we might convince ourselves that we are superior to other groups. We might even come to believe that people in other groups are somehow less than human.

But on both sides of any stereotype, any conflict, or any war, we are *all* human. We want the same things, regardless of our external differences. All of us want peace, security inside and out, and the chance to give and receive love.

Recently I took a trip to Israel—a land that has been filled with ethnic and religious hatred for centuries. There are so many groups attacking different groups for different reasons, I can't imagine how anyone could feel safe there. For years, I have been reading about the dangers, the suicide bombings, the retaliation. So I expected to see evidence of great fear. But while I was there, I learned something else about the way people were feeling.

We traveled around the country on a tour bus in the intense summer heat. At the first stop, I only spent about thirty minutes outside the bus before I realized I needed to get some relief. While my tour mates were seeing the sights, I ducked into an air-conditioned cafeteria.

It was about eleven in the morning. As I was figuring out how to order coffee, I noticed our bus driver in the cafeteria, having lunch by himself. I had met him only about an hour earlier, when he picked us up at the airport. He was a handsome man in his mid-forties with a dark, ruddy complexion, black hair, and deep brown eyes. The bus he was driving was an old model with a clumsy wheelchair lift; this driver had been very helpful about guiding me onto the lift and into the bus.

Now, seated in the cafeteria, he was eating alone, staring absentmindedly as he picked at his food. He seemed pleased when I asked if I could sit with him.

I learned that his name was Marwan and he was a Christian Arab from Nazareth. He told me he lived by himself. He eked out a living by driving a bus, and worried about taking care of his ailing mother. And he told me that since the death of Arafat, he had felt like he could "smell peace."

· · ·

Later that week, I was to hear that same phrase from the lips of an Israeli. Even if they could not yet see it or feel it, peace was something that people could smell.

What else were people feeling?

I had the opportunity to raise that question with an Israeli psychologist, Yovav Katz, host of a call-in radio show in Jerusalem that has been running more than twenty-five years. What did his callers want to talk about? Even as I asked, I was fairly certain of Yovav's reply. Surely he would tell me that they wanted to talk about terrorism or the economy.

Instead, he replied, "Loneliness."

Yovav observed that although there was much poverty in Israel, the percentage of very wealthy people had steadily increased in the past decade. In his view, those with wealth tended to be more self-absorbed, which inevitably leads to loneliness. I shared my own perspective—that people are lonely because there is something missing in their lives. People with wealth try to compensate by accumulating things, but it's not a lack of *things* that makes people lonely. What was happening here?

I think I got my answer the next night.

The group from my tour bus had dinner at a beautiful restaurant overlooking the Sea of Galilee. Afterward, everyone else went on a boat ride. I stayed back and had coffee with Marwan, who was starting to trust me. He interrupted the silence by asking, "Have you ever been in love?"

I said that I had.

There was a long pause. Then Marwan told me a story

of the woman he had loved for eleven years. One day, on her way to work, the woman he loved had been killed in a car accident. Ten years had passed, and still he mourned. He said he had never gone out with another woman because he never met "the right one." What he meant was he had never found the woman he lost. His grief was palpable because he had loved and been loved so deeply.

A few days later, when I talked again with Marwan (who now called me "my brother"), I asked him what he thought his lover would say if she came back for just five minutes. He sat quietly for a long time as his eyes welled up with tears. "I don't know," he said finally. "Maybe she would say she misses me too. Maybe she would say she doesn't want me to suffer any more because she loves me." And, maybe for the first time, he wept.

Marwan is not the only one who is mourning. I thought about all the people I have seen over the years who have suffered the loss of loved ones. I thought about all the tears that Jew and Arab alike have shed. I wondered how many of those tears had turned to hatred. What I learned in Israel was that, maybe, underneath all of the hatred and rage, was shared human pain. Centuries of grief for all the losses— and centuries of longing for simple peace, security inside and out, and the chance to love and be loved.

At President Clinton's first inauguration, Maya Angelou read a poem that contained these lines: "History, despite its wrenching pain,/cannot be unlived, and if faced/with courage, need not be lived again." With so many people living every day with the wrenching pain of history, Sam, I wish more of them could smell peace. Perhaps they could find a way to see it and feel it too.

Perhaps, in your life, you'll find a way to help them.

Love,
Pop

———

BEING "PRODUCTIVE"

Dear Sam,

Not long ago, I gave a panel presentation on the topic of disabilities. One of my guests had written a best-selling book called *Riding the Bus with My Sister*. The sister, who had a developmental disability, was able to function independently (with some minor help) but unable to work. Instead, she rode the bus all day, just talking with people.

One of the women in the audience, a college professor, raised her hand. She wanted to talk about whether the young woman riding the bus—the sister with disabilities—was "being productive." The question made me angry and I told the professor why. Here's what I said:

"We live in a world that seems to be lacking kindness and compassion. It looks to me as if our world has too much hatred, judgment, and aggression. Most of us 'productive' people work hard, pay the bills, maybe send a check to charity every now and then, and go home and watch reality TV. How many people in the audience bring pleasure to the lives of another living being every day?"

. . .

Some time ago, Sam, I was treating a woman in her late fifties who was severely depressed. Her mother, in her early eighties, had just moved into this woman's house. Since the older woman was incapacitated, I did something I rarely have time to do. I went to their home.

Early in the session, I asked the mother to describe her daughter.

"Oh, she's an angel!" said the older woman.

My patient reacted with a plastic-looking smile. "No, Mom, I'm really not. I'm just a person."

"No, no—you're an angel. An absolute angel!"

Thinking we'd better move on, I asked the mother what life was like for her. She talked about how frustrated she felt at being dependent. She couldn't help her daughter make beds the way she used to. She couldn't clean the house, do the laundry, or wash dishes. "I feel so worthless!" she told me.

So the daughter was doing all these tasks that her mother could no longer do. She really didn't seem to mind. But her mother sure did. She was angry because she wasn't "productive." Her daughter continually tried to reassure her mother that it was all right, but that didn't seem to help very much.

So I asked the daughter how her mother *could* be most helpful.

"I wish Mom would just sit with me and talk," she said. "All of our lives together, either she was too busy to listen to me or I was too busy to listen to her. So I never felt as though my mother knew me for who I really was. She just saw me as 'perfect.' Now that we both have time, I would like to just sit with her and tell her the story of who I am. And I'm thinking maybe I could hear her story too."

I saw the reflective look in her mother's eyes as she replied simply, "I could do that."

So what does it mean to be productive? We must feed, clothe, and house ourselves and our loved ones. Are we productive when we do the dishes and laundry? Clean the house? I suppose so. But what if we just sit with someone and show compassion?

Sam, for me a productive day looks much the same as any other. I wake up alert, and I get my work done. I write a column or see patients. But at a deeper level, I finish my day with more energy and aliveness if I truly feel that at least part of my day has contributed to someone else's welfare. I don't need to change the world. But the day is better when I am able to share an intimate moment with someone, listen in a way someone has not been listened to before, or tell a story that gets someone thinking differently. Then I feel my day is productive, and I feel grateful for having lived it.

When I think about the woman who rides the bus, I believe there's a good chance she brings pleasure to people's lives every hour of every day. So I wouldn't encourage anyone to ask whether she is "productive."

Sam, you and I need help throughout our lives, and we depend on people's compassion. So we have to teach people that being compassionate not only feels good, not only helps us, but will also make the world a kinder and safer place. When you show compassion—and when you receive it—you *are* being productive. I hope no one will be able to convince you otherwise.

Love,
Pop

YOU AND YOUR TIGER

Dear Sam,

Not long ago, I read a book called *Life of Pi*. It was about a sixteen-year-old boy who became a castaway on a lifeboat. His sole companion on that boat was a 450-pound Bengal tiger! Pi found himself on top of a piece of tarpaulin with the tiger underneath. For months, they floated on the ocean.

Pi had to work out some kind of a relationship with this tiger. He knew the tiger could easily kill him, but he could not kill the tiger. He also knew he could not control or tame the tiger. And there they were floating on the ocean together!

Though Pi was starving, there was no way he could overpower the big cat and eat it. In fact, the only way he could preserve his own life was by feeding the tiger. He found a way to catch fish and share them with his four-footed constant companion. When he found a way to purify water, that too he shared.

Somehow they lived in this fragile, frightening, mutually dependent relationship for many months as their boat floated, unguided, across the ocean. As soon as the lifeboat washed ashore, the tiger ran away into the jungle.

And Pi cried.

Do you know why?

The story of Pi is the story of all of us. We all have tigers under our tarpaulins—tigers that, we feel, could destroy us. We think we want to be rid of our tigers. But the truth is, we would feel a great loss if they ran away, because ultimately, each tiger is a part of us.

Jerome Groopman, M.D., a physician at Harvard Medical School and a staff writer for *The New Yorker*, tells a story about his own tiger in a book called *The Anatomy of Hope*. Groopman relates that he suffered with severe back pain for many years. As the pain got worse, he accommodated it more. He didn't pick up his children when they were small, he tried not to walk long distances, and he would lie down for several hours each day with an ice pack on his back. And still the pain increased.

One day, Groopman went to see a doctor who specialized in rehabilitation medicine. The doctor told Groopman that he had been worshiping at the altar of pain for all those years. As he negotiated with the gods of pain, he offered an appeasement that went something like this: "If I accommodate you in this way, then maybe you won't hurt me so badly."

Groopman realized that as he accommodated the pain, it persisted. And the more he accommodated, the more it demanded.

I think many of us do this with our tigers. If the tiger is fear of rejection, we might not get into an intimate relationship. If the tiger is depression, we might stay home more and socialize less. If it's insecurity, we might devote our lives to appearing more productive than everyone else, just to hide from that tiger.

When his doctor told him not to worship at that altar anymore, Groopman stopped accommodating and began living the life he was given.

Want to know one of your pop's tigers? There was a time in my life when I was severely depressed and felt like my mind was ill. I was scared to be in groups because I thought my ill mind was visible. Each morning when I woke up, I would try to figure out how many hours I had to get through before I could go back to bed.

My tiger was depression. It still is. So when I feel slightly depressed, which happens pretty often, I can get really scared. I get anxious and begin thinking of what I can do about it and how quickly. The issue is not the tiger. The issue is the fear.

The truth is, if I were to get seriously depressed again, it would be awful, but I would get treatment and get better. Yes, I am frightened about my depression, but I don't live my life in continual fear of it, because I have learned that faith helps to cure fear. Today I have faith that I can tolerate my painful emotions. I have faith that if and when my depression comes back, it will be temporary. And I'll be able to live with it.

Groopman never got over the back pain. He still endured it every day. But after he talked with that doctor and realized what the pain was doing to him, he made sure it no longer dominated his life.

. . .

Sam, everyone has demons inside. Psychoanalyst Carl Jung called them our "shadows." He meant that we have parts of ourselves that we can't deal with. But we can't run away or separate ourselves from them. The shadows are part of us.

Like Pi, you will have tigers—emotions and impulses that you are afraid of. They may take the face of depression, compulsiveness, dependency, aggression, hatred, or envy. But if you cannot destroy them, outsmart them, or run away from them, what can you do about them?

Our tigers are not monsters. They are just parts of ourselves that have long been ignored, seeking a voice. Welcome them, feed them, and listen to what they have to say. There is really not a whole lot to be afraid of. After all, everything you find in there is a part of Sam. What could be better?

Love,
Pop

———

A LESSON IN DYING

Dear Sam,

One day you will die. And the more you enjoy your life, the less you will want this to happen.

But death is not your enemy. Knowing that your life has an endpoint will help you appreciate every moment you're alive. Death helps you understand life's precious gifts.

We fight against death because each of us has an unbelievable drive for survival. That's why death is so difficult—because we love life the way we do. But almost everyone reaches a point where they give up the fight. Some of these people have been my best teachers.

Shortly after your Aunt Sharon was diagnosed with a terminal illness, I got a call from a woman named Caroline who asked if she could see me for therapy. When she told me she had pancreatic cancer, I knew that she was dealing with a terminal disease. But at that point, none of the doctors had told her so. She didn't quite know yet that her death was imminent.

If I had taken a more traditional view of the doctor-patient relationship, I probably would have declined to treat Caroline. I was dealing with my own sister's impending death—and your great-grandmother and great-grandfather were unwell, so I knew I'd be losing them too. But I agreed to see her.

When Caroline came in, I asked what she wanted to work on. She told me she wanted to improve her relationship with her mother. She also wanted to be more assertive in other relationships. I said, "I'll help you with that stuff. But if and when the time comes, you have to help me with this death thing—because soon I'm going to be facing death in my own family. So when the time comes, you'll be my teacher."

It worked just that way. At first we explored her relationship with her mother, tracking its history and beginning to repair some wounds. As our relationship developed, she began to talk about the experience of having cancer and how hard she was working with diet, exercise, and chemotherapy to keep the disease at bay.

After her second CAT scan, Caroline came into my office knowing that her battle with cancer was over. She was a whole different person with a whole different face. It was as though she had crossed some kind of threshold and found herself at peace.

Sam, a wise person once said that all children are born knowing what the angels look like. I have come to believe it's so. And those angels may come along later in life to remind us of their presence. When Caroline walked into my office that evening, she knew what the angels looked like.

This shy, demure woman who never asserted herself now told me that she wanted to bring in her pregnant daughter and talk to her. That's what she did. Frail, ailing,

Caroline put her arms around her daughter and reassured her that after she died, she would watch out for her.

As long as she had strength enough to come to my office, she continued to do so. We talked about life and death. She told me what it felt like to be dying and how she was both saying good-bye to her past while experiencing every moment and every breath with light and gratitude.

A few weeks later, in the middle of the night, I got a call from Caroline's daughter. She said, "It's time."

I asked the daughter to hold the phone to her mother's ear, which she did.

"Caroline," I asked, "how are you?"

That's a funny thing to ask a dying woman, but she said, "I'm fine."

"Caroline, you did your job well," I told her.

"I know."

We told each other that we loved each other, and we said good-bye. She died a few hours later.

Caroline was a landscape architect. A week after she died, I gave a lecture at a local hospital well known for its gardens. I was given a thank-you gift of azaleas, which I planted outside my office window. That's where Caroline is to me now.

Caroline taught me that when we stop fighting against death, we are able to wake up to our lives. I hope I never forget that lesson. And I hope you never do.

Love,
Pop

———

MAKE THE CONTAINER BIGGER

Dear Sam,

Sometimes when I'm watching you, I see worry cross your face. That expression tells me that things aren't going quite the way you'd like them to, and that your world is out of order. Sometimes I feel like I would do almost anything to make your pain go away, but that wouldn't be a very good idea. One thing all children need is resilience, and you need it more than most. Without resilience, the slightest adversity in life can feel enormous and debilitating. And the best way to build resilience in adulthood is by facing adversity and learning from it in childhood. The important thing is not avoiding problems; it's learning how to cope with them.

Most people want their problems to go away quickly because problems make them feel uncomfortable or sad. It is in the nature of pain—physical or emotional—to demand our attention. It's as though the pain is telling us there is something wrong that needs to be repaired. But that attention is like sticking your tongue in a cavity or becoming preoccupied with an emotional problem. Sometimes the attention itself just makes the pain worse. Your field of vision narrows, and you begin to think you and your problem are bigger and more important than they really are.

Although some acute problems can be fixed, like the toothache I just mentioned, or a broken bone, many problems we may just have to find a way to live with. But how can we live with a problem that might cause us physical or emotional pain? One way is to look at our problem through a wider lens.

There's a story from Zen tradition about a young student who is suffering so terribly, he can't get a moment's rest. So he goes to his master to ask for help.

The teacher advises him to put a tablespoon of coarse salt in a glass of water, stir it around, and drink it down. The student does as he's told. Of course the water tastes terribly salty.

"Now," says the teacher, indicating a spring that's bubbling from the ground, "I want you to pour a tablespoon of salt into the spring water." The student does. When the master instructs him to drink the spring water, the student finds that the taste of salt is imperceptible.

"The problem is not the salt," says the master. "The problem is the container. You have to make the container bigger."

Some time ago, I treated a woman who suffered from depression. I had sent her to a psychiatrist who prescribed medication, but when she started taking it, she suffered badly from the side effects and had to stop. He tried again with a different kind of medication, and again she had terrible side effects.

She was quite motivated to deal with this depression, so—frustrating though it was—she kept trying different medications with the same results. In her sessions with me, she began talking about leaving her job. In a way, I supported this decision, because her job was immensely stressful and making her depression worse. However, leaving a job can be dangerous for someone who's already depressed. It can lead to further isolation and worsen the depression. I felt I was in a difficult position about whether to support her leaving. Either way felt wrong.

Finally, I told her that I would agree to her leaving the job if, when she did, she would begin to devote twenty hours a week to some kind of community service. But her community service had to be something more than addressing envelopes or making phone calls on behalf of a social cause. It had to be something that brought her in direct contact with living beings who would benefit from her help.

She readily agreed to the deal. She volunteered to spend ten hours a week as a part-time librarian in an elementary school, reading to children. For another ten hours each week, she prepared and delivered meals to people with AIDS. Very soon, she came back and told me she was meeting nice people, making new friends. (That's important for all of us, but especially for people with depression.) And the friends she was making were good people—the kind of people who cared about others. This made these new friendships even more valuable.

More weeks passed, and she reported that she was beginning to care deeply about those she was helping. For the first time in years, she was feeling good about herself and her life.

After two or three months, I could see she was still depressed, though somewhat less so. So I referred her back to her psychiatrist for medication. And this time she was able to tolerate it better. Her body chemistry had actually changed!

In the years since I "made the deal" with that woman, I have treated many patients who seem terribly self-absorbed and isolated with their problems. For the sake of their mental health, I often give them advice that takes them far away from the office where we're sitting. Typically, I may ask them to devote two hours a week to help a person or animal. They might volunteer at an animal shelter, day-care center, or old-age home. The choice is theirs. But usually when people accept this deal, and follow through, they tell me the experience has changed their lives.

Making the container bigger can change the world from the inside out. Very often, people who step outside of themselves and begin helping others wind up getting better more quickly. They become part of the larger world. Their own problems no longer fill it up.

Your problems will never vanish, Sam. Neither you nor

I can "wish away" the distress you sometimes feel. And you cannot turn your back on your own suffering. But if you step out into the world, I think you will find that the container is much, much bigger than you had imagined.

Love,
Pop

———

YOUR BIRTHDAY GIFT TO ME

Dear Sam,

I'm writing this letter to you at the shore. When I came out of my room this morning and started planning my day in my head, I didn't pay attention to the ocean or the waves. But outside the waves formed out on a quiet sea, a hundred yards from shore. Moving steadily, these waves broke onto the beach, while, a hundred yards out, new ones were taking form.

All this continued while I was busy planning my day and listing the calls I had to make. The waves went unnoticed. So did the smells in the air and the sounds around me. So did my breath. And genuine emotions went by unnoticed too. How long would it be, in the midst of my multitasking, before my life went unnoticed?

Sam, the most powerful lesson I learned about noticing came on your last birthday.

Your father had been telling me for months that you were a good little golfer. And enthusiastic. He even got you your own set of golf clubs. I was delighted when I heard how much you liked the game. And then along came your birthday—and you and your father invited me to go on the golf course with you. I was overcome with emotion. That's because I had not been on a golf course since my accident twenty-five years ago.

Before I became a quadriplegic, I loved to play golf. My father, like yours, taught me how to play, and it was our way of being close. Once he and I were on the golf course, I knew I would be spending several hours alone with him. Those were important occasions.

After my accident, my grief about golf was so painful that I couldn't drive past a course without feeling tearful. So when you and your dad invited me, I felt a little uncomfortable. But mostly I was eager to see you and your dad play.

When you and your dad and I got on the course, I was relieved that I was able to navigate the turf in my wheelchair. Then I experienced all over again the beauty of that environment. I had forgotten how wonderful a golf course smells and the magnificence of the manicured lawns, dotted with sand traps, that seem to go on forever.

I saw you put the ball down and take a swing. Your form was beautiful. You connected with the ball. I can't ever remember feeling such pride and gratitude. I was almost giddy with joy as we made our way down the fairway.

And then I began to think. I thought about how much I would love to be able to swing a club myself and feel the grass under my feet. Instantly I was overcome with pain. If I had been alone, I would have wept. I remembered how a golf club used to feel in my hand. For the first time in years, I allowed myself to wish for something I could not have.

A few minutes later, as I noticed you were taking a golf club out of your bag, I reminded myself where I was. Again I took in the grandeur, watched you hit the ball, and felt great joy. You lofted the ball about twenty yards and all three of us applauded your accomplishment.

Once again, I felt joyous and exhilarated. So I began thinking about whether or not we could adapt a golf club to my hand . . . and maybe I could swing from my wheel-chair . . . and maybe . . .

And then I realized that whatever we did, it wouldn't feel like it did before. It would probably feel clumsy and not much fun. More sadness and more grief.

Then your little voice snapped me out of my painful reverie. I heard you say to your father, "Great shot, Dad!" Again I felt joy and gratitude as I took in all that was around me.

Sam, when I lived in the present moment with you, noticing what was happening in that moment, I felt great joy. When my mind went to the past and what I had lost, I felt pain. When my mind went to the future and what I longed for, I felt pain then too.

So many of us grown-ups suffer because we are trying to live the life we once had or the life we wish for. You reminded me that day that life is much sweeter when we live the life we have.

Thank you.

Love,
Pop

AFTERWORD

SAYING GOOD-BYE

Dear Sam,

How do we end a book like this?

I am writing this last letter more than four years after the first one, which welcomed you to the world. When you were nearly four years old, with the help of intensive speech therapy, you began to talk. And now it seems almost like you are making up for lost time! The more you talk, the more your mom, dad, and I understand the kind of boy you are. Sure, you still have lots of autistic symptoms, like difficulty with fine motor skills, some rigid behaviors, social clumsiness, and a speech impediment, but you have blossomed into a caring, sensitive, and happy (not to mention beautiful) child. Whenever we see each other, you climb on my lap and we take a ride in my wheelchair and talk.

Your mother told me recently that when you were coming to visit me once, you saw industrial smokestacks and said, "Mommy, look at those cloud machines." Your eyes, your mind, and your heart are all open and thirsty. And as you continue your therapies, you develop new abilities every day. So now I have lots of hope that you will be able to pick up this book and read these letters for yourself.

. . .

We started this book by saying hello to a precious life, so we must end it by saying good-bye to one.

I have been near death several times and, as a result, I almost always feel it to be nearby. But, Sam, I have long believed that death is not a problem. *Not living* is the problem. Sadness, joy, love, anguish, passion, and serenity are all pieces of life—the very texture of this gift called life. In a wonderful poem called "Guest House," the Sufi poet Rūmī challenges us to welcome all those emotions, all those sorrows and joys, into our being. "Meet them at the door laughing," he tells us, "and invite them in."

After I'm gone, your heart will be broken, and there will be a missing piece there. Over time, as I've told you in this book, your heart will heal, because that's what hearts do. You will still miss me, but when you think of me, I hope you will feel more love and happiness than sadness.

If, as I have dreamed, you have read this book all the way to the end, then this is where we part. This book, for me, has been a gift all around. It's my gift to you, to my daughters, and to those who might read it. To me it has been a gift to have the opportunity, the ability, the where-withal to put in writing some of my stories and my dreams and fears for you. But despite all the work and despite the fact that I have been thinking about things like this my whole life, there is so much I haven't communicated and cannot communicate to you. Because many of my deepest emotions are beyond words.

What I want to communicate to you is the feeling we

get in our hearts when we gaze deeply into the eyes of someone we have loved for a long time. I want to convey the emotional dance of tearfulness and sadness and intimacy—all beyond words.

As you put down this book, I want it to be like you and me gazing deeply into each other's eyes. I leave you that as my final gift.

Love,
Pop

———

GUEST HOUSE

This being human is a guest house
Every morning a new arrival.
A joy, a depression, a meanness,
some momentary awareness comes
as an unexpected visitor.
Welcome and entertain them all!
Even if they are a crowd of sorrows,
who violently sweep your house
empty of its furniture,
still treat each guest honorably.
He may be clearing you out for some new delight.
The dark thought, the sham, the malice,
meet them at the door laughing,
and invite them in.
Be grateful for whoever comes,
because each has been sent
as a guide from beyond.

—*Rūmī*

RESOURCES

For more information about autism:

Center for the Study of Autism
http://www.autism.org

Yale Developmental Disabilities Clinic
http://info.med.yale.edu/chldstdy/autism/

Cure Autism Now
http://www.cureautismnow.org/

Help and advice for families with children on the spectrum:

Alternative Choices
http://www.specialfamilies.com/specialfamilies.htm

For adults coping with disability:

National Spinal Cord Injury Association:
http://www.spinalcord.org/

To help make the world a more loving place for children,
contribute or volunteer at programs like:

Boys and Girls Clubs of America
http://www.bgca.org

Big Brothers Big Sisters
http://www.bbbsa.org/

World Centers of Compassion for Children International
http://www.centersofcompassion.org

To reach Dr. Dan directly:
http://www.DrDanGottlieb.com

ACKNOWLEDGMENTS

Fifteen years ago I was introduced to Ed Claflin and was told he was a pretty good writer. He is much more than a good writer; he is a good editor and a good agent. He is a man with a kind heart and one of my closest friends.

Special thanks to Tracy Schwartz, a young woman I have known since she went to camp with my daughter Debbie over twenty years ago. As a relatively new employee at Sterling, she told me she thought it would be a good idea if "the guy I work for" read my proposal. Boy, was it! I could not have asked for a publishing house with more commitment and more integrity. In my editor, Patty Gift, not only do I have someone with talent and vision, I also have someone who is a kindred spirit.

This book could not have been written had I not survived this demanding disability over this past quarter century. For that I thank my doctors, my genetics, and my stubbornness. But I especially thank the nurses who come to my home every day and care for and about me.

Twenty years ago, WHYY radio in Philadelphia took a gamble on an insecure wheelchair-bound psychologist who had a pretty unusual take on life. Their gamble turned into my treasure. Several years later, the *Philadelphia Inquirer* offered me a column. And between the two, I have been given a voice in my community. Both of these institutions have contributed enormously to the quality of my life and the clarity of my mind. For these gifts, I am both honored and grateful.

Maiken Scott has been my producer at WHYY for many years. Over that time, I have come to trust and admire her. She has been very helpful in my organizing and publicizing this work. I have come to know her as an excellent producer, a wonderful friend, and a deeply caring human being.

My gratitude to the Templeton Foundation and their initial financial support for this book when it was not much more than a quiet voice of devotion to a little boy.

Rachel Simon, the gifted author of *Riding the Bus with My Sister,* and Maiken Scott, my radio producer, have been enormously helpful in getting this book into people's hands.

Robert Naseef is a good friend and colleague and served as a guide throughout the writing and publicizing of this book.

My deepest thanks is reserved for all of my teachers, the individuals, couples, and families who have come to my office over the last three decades, people who have shared their pain, opened their hearts, and honored me with their trust. I cannot imagine a better venue in which to learn the lessons about what it means to be human.

To some of my earliest mentors, Alfred Friedman, Geraldine Grossman, Gertrude Cohen, Jeff Marks, Oscar Wiener, Carl Rogers, and Karl Whitaker. To the thousands of brilliant people I have met over the years through my radio show and columns.

Dr. Michael Baime, an internist and teacher at the University of Pennsylvania introduced me to mindfulness meditation and Buddhist thinking ten years ago. We have become friends but he continues to be my teacher.

How blessed one is who can look to their past and feel nothing but love and gratitude. My parents, Jack and Betty Gottlieb, were not special. They were just kind, loving, and devoted parents. How lucky I was to have them. How much I miss them.

Readers of this book already know something about my sister Sharon, but there is much more I would tell if I could. She was special. She was a community leader, a woman who walked the walk when it came to women's rights and many other social justice issues, my great supporter, my closest friend and my role model. Sometimes, when I feel confused and everything is still, I continue to feel her guidance.

My niece Chelsey, her aunt Amy, and her sister Katie have deepened my life and expanded my vision of what family really means

The moment I laid eyes on my firstborn daughter, Ali, I made a solemn promise to love and care for her every moment of every day for the rest of her life. I made that same promise eleven months later when Debbie was born. I have made lots of promises, and broken most of them, but these I've kept. It's been easy: I have two daughters who have provided me with great love, pride, and purpose. There are no words for my love and gratitude for these wonderful young women.

You have read on these pages how I missed Sandy when our marriage deteriorated, when she left, and when she died. I ached for her company when Sam was born. How much she would have enjoyed playing with Sam and watching our child become a wonderful mother. How much I would have enjoyed watching Sandy watch Sam. And now I miss her again as I end these letters to our grandson.

Royalities from the sale of this book are being donated to Cure Autism Now and other children's charities.